MAKING A
DIFFERENCE
2.0

MAKING A DIFFERENCE 2.0

The Ultimate Guide to Online Charitable Giving

HOWARD FREEMAN

Skyhorse Publishing

Skyhorse Publishing books may be purchased in bulk at special discounts for sales promotion, corporate gifts, fund-raising, or educational purposes. Special editions can also be created to specifications. For details, contact the Special Sales Department, Skyhorse Publishing, 307 West 36th Street, 11th Floor, New York, NY 10018 or info@ skyhorsepublishing.com.

Skyhorse® and Skyhorse Publishing® are registered trademarks of Skyhorse Publishing, Inc.®, a Delaware corporation.

Visit our website at www.skyhorsepublishing.com.

10 9 8 7 6 5 4 3 2 1

Library of Congress Cataloging-in-Publication Data is available on file.

ISBN: 978-1-61608-748-7

Printed in the United States of America

To the Moms in my life.
They have always defined generosity for me,
online and off.

Contents

Acknowledgments

Thanks first go to Tony Lyons at Skyhorse Publishing for his vision for a fundraising book and his support of this project. Zoey Creative Development advisors Scott Kauffmann, Bill Levin, and Andrew Wallace-Barnett have been pillars. Much of the research led to interviews with industry leaders, whom I'm grateful to for their time and insights: Rob Wu and Jeff Chang of CauseVox; Hugh Evans, Michael Trainer and Elisha London of Global Poverty Project; Jackie Jensen and Joe Henriod of Ticket Cake; Jeffrey DiGangi; Phil McCarty of GoodScoutGroup; Erik Lokkesmoe and Tyler Michel of Different Drummer; Jay Walsh of Wikimedia Foundation; Tania Major, Michael Bouy and Ian Ryder, fellow fundraisers based in Australia; Jay Harren of Downtime; and Elkin Antoniou and Bobby Garabedian for walking through the minefields of taking a music video into the online giving world. The Hewlett Foundation compiled an excellent spreadsheet that exhaustively outlines what the platforms are. Our research booted off of theirs. Paul Penley of Intelligent Philanthropy first told me about the Hewlett report, and I am indebted to him. Huge thanks to Cory Allyn at Skyhorse for his invaluable assistance and unwavering patience. Gavin French was a superb research associate. Daryl Heald taught me in 2002 what generosity looked like, but I didn't quite get it until a year later. My three sons get props for not groaning too much about my having the very "uncool" job of fundraiser. My wife deserves a big hug and more than a few hours face time for putting up with my long hours spent in front of the glow of a computer screen instead of basking in her light.

Introduction

WHY ARE YOU READING THIS BOOK?

My youngest son, then five, was walking with me on Broadway in New York City near our apartment. We passed a man sitting against an iron fence in front of a church, holding a cardboard sign with black letters that spelled out his need. I'd seen this man before; he was almost a fixture in our neighborhood. My son walked a few steps farther, looking back while holding my hand before turning to at me and asking, "Can I have my allowance now?"

"Why … sure," I replied. It was a dollar.

He took the bill and walked over to the man and dropped it into his bucket. Trotting back, my son grabbed my hand again and we kept walking. Me, the proud father, the philanthropy expert no less, with my Generous Progeny.

A few steps later, he looked up again. "Dad?"

"Yes?"

"Can I have another dollar?"

Perhaps you gave some money to a homeless person because you wanted to. Or you didn't because you had your reasons. Or you did because you wanted to avoid the guilt of not doing so. Any way you slice it, giving is a choice. It's voluntary, and so it should be.

It's different from taxes, different from buying, and different from saving and then giving through your estate.

With the Internet, giving is a choice saturated with a consumer look and feel. This is not necessarily bad. It is sometimes an entry point, a way into the world of philanthropy that, once engaged in, can lead to greater giving and a greater common good. Voluntary giving has to compete against other choices we make with our money, and it's not always clear what that competition is.

Whether you're a professional fundraiser starting or building your online giving program, a volunteer helping a cause by raising money from your friends and peers, or a newcomer looking to make a financial donation online, this guide will walk you through some of the technical aspects behind the gift of giving, as well as illustrate the best practices and examples of those who are doing online giving well. You'll understand who nonprofits really compete against and how we can cast a vision for our online givers. Further, this guide will paint a picture of the kind of community that the best online giving requires as well as the community the best online giving creates.

IRL (In Real Life): "Live Below the Line"

Though I've been in fundraising for almost seventeen years, I'd never asked for money from friends for a project I was personally (not professionally) involved in. In 1986, I did a walk-a-thon in New York City but signed up my sponsors to pledge by the mile run, not the mile walked. I ran the last ten miles in old sneakers. I couldn't press my feet to the ground the next day, so I used some sick time. That was it; my personal fundraising episode, until my next experience nearly twenty-five years later, also involving personal discomfort but on a more modest scale.

In May 2011, I joined thousands of others in the "Live Below the Line" campaign organized by the Global Poverty Project (GPP). The "line" is a daily budget of $1.50, below which 1.4 billion people live. Sometimes an entire family lives on this amount for all needs, but I was to do this alone and use only for food— my wife and kids would continue as normal. But for those doing LBL, we were being reminded for five days of the desperate need of those living in extreme poverty. So were our supporters. The idea was not to make us feel poor so much as to transform each of us to do something more once the challenge had ended.

Let me outline how GPP was able to accomplish this goal, as a micro-fundraiser for them. It

3

was a combination of offline and online work, a solo effort as well as one with teams. And they spread it across multiple nations.

A year earlier, I had attended a mid-sized reception and presentation where about 200 people shared hors d'oeuvres and enjoyed cocktails in an amazing downtown New York City space. Actor Hugh Jackman emceed. We heard GPP founder Hugh Evans tell his story and call us to take a simple action. *Would we "Like" their Facebook page? Or write a letter to a politician? Or make a donation? And would we do it that night?* So here was a wonderful evening, to which I was invited by a friend and where I thoroughly enjoyed myself and heard an amazing story. What was my response?

I recall taking the path of least resistance: I went home and "Liked" the GPP Facebook page, delegating it to the electronic attic of fan pages alongside the TV show "House," my favorite dead authors, and "Brother Jimmy's" barbecue

restaurant. In other words, I clicked "Like" on Facebook, got a laboratory animal-like boost of altruistic endorphins shooting through my body, and then I went away.

But GPP did not go away. They used my "Like" skillfully.

Many "Likes" on cultural items both great and small later, I got a Facebook event invitation with a link to a video, seen here. I was impressed by the quality of the video, and it didn't hurt to have an X-Man pitching me (In fact, I bet you clicked over just now, if you didn't already). I received another and probably a third, asking me to consider the LBL event. At one point, I just thought, "What the hey. Sure." So I signed up to do it.

In the week before the LBL "fast," I was supposed to raise money. I'd never minded raising money on behalf of an organization before, but I didn't like the prospect of asking someone to "sponsor me." A rejection would be way too personal. It was a bit intimidating. Yet once I jumped I didn't look back. I reminded myself first and foremost why I was doing it: the money would go towards initiatives to reduce extreme poverty in various parts of the world. Once I got over the "why" part, it was fairly straightforward.

So I kicked off my fundraising effort by:

• Creating a LBL Campaign Facebook banner.

• Being the first donor (Can't ask others to do what you haven't done yourself).

• Doing something I had never done before: I sent an appeal email to everyone on my email list. Everyone. Putting them in the bcc: line. And I said so in the first line of my note. Something like, "I know getting a note where your name is bcc:ed is kind of impersonal, but this is going to everyone in my contact list. I have never done this before, but I need everyone's help. I need *your*

help…" and it went from there. Again, it was in alignment with answering my "why" question: if my efforts were designed to help alleviate extreme poverty, I was more than glad to ask everyone I knew, even if a few people got angry. (One person of my roughly 1,200 contacts emailed me and expressed doubt about this "attempt to get people to experience true poverty." I sent him back my reasoning on why this was different, and then I happened to see him, and we had a good discussion.)

At the end of two days of fundraising, our team was first out of more than 3,000 U.S. teams, and we completed the campaign in that position. I had some eighty donors who gave gifts ranging between $10 and $250. The site listed the top ten fundraisers, and being competitive… I was *determined* to finish first! My son's karate teacher calls this "friendly competition." But the story is a testimony to the donors and to the vision of eradicating extreme poverty.

So, what other online and offline actions helped?

- I made YouTube videos and circulated them to supporters and potential donors.

- LBL/GPP staff constantly encouraged me. They even mailed me a Crumpler shoulder bag as a present on the second or third day of the campaign (offline perks like this can make a difference when the donor doesn't expect it). They published on their site a photo of me wearing the bag and standing next to my son. Very fun.

- I sent daily email updates to supporters during the fast itself through the LBL email system, which made it easy to send to all or send to those who had donated since a certain date.

- I made sure to personally thank supporters immediately after receiving notice of their gifts (GPP allowed us to insert our email address so that we would get gift alerts).

- I thanked supporters multiple times and told them what food I had bought with the money and about my culinary skills (or lack thereof). I kept it all lighthearted, so they'd keep reading. I told them occasionally about the work of GPP and encouraged them to click over to the GPP website to learn more. By the end of the campaigns, one of my supporters said he was persuaded to take his whole family of five through the experience!

- I asked supporters to share the campaign with their friends.

- I used and perhaps overused Facebook and Twitter, and I shamelessly and (I hope) somewhat humorously promoted myself as the number one fundraising team in order to get more donations. I received only a handful of gifts from people who weren't my friends, but I was pulling out all the stops and didn't mind if this was considered a bit aggressive. Frankly, I was willing to look like an idiot to get more money to help the cause.

- I was into it 100%. Online and offline. "All in."

Here's what I learned:

- A short campaign is sustainable for volunteer micro-fundraisers. This one required sustained attention for about three weeks.

- An upbeat nonprofit staff that encouraged everyone made a big difference. They responded to my messages promptly, even before I had raised much money at all. *They were "all in" and into it 100%.*

- As a volunteer micro-fundraiser, you can definitely appeal to your entire mailing list for something you really believe in and want to do...but it's like castling in chess. You can only do it once per game.

- Online campaigns can be—and should be—lots of fun because of the nature of the tools at our disposal.

- This video of Gillian Zinser from Beverly Hills 90210 talking about giving up her 'soy frappuccino whatever whatever,' and one of a guy in Austin, Texas, who lived in his car for a week...on $1.50 per day, period—food, drinks, everything—made it a collective experience that bound me with TV stars and Wolverine and a poor dude living in his car in Austin. It felt like, "C'mon, everyone! Join the party!" GPP found a way to always inspire their fundraisers.

- Facebook and Twitter got lit up, and the ever-present hashtag of #LBLUSA kept everyone on social media all week during our fast.

- To underscore <u>one thing I learned more than anything</u>: I have an amazing bunch of friends and acquaintances. I relied on that community to come through for the cause, and they overwhelmingly did. The community in my address book is what made it happen.

7

Elisha London, U.K. Country Director for GPP, told me that while fundraising is one part of the "Live Below the Line" challenge, the core goal is to engage.

"We hear and talk about extreme poverty a lot, which is good," she said, "but to go further than this and take a five-day journey…individuals are changed dramatically. We want to take people on [that] journey. People blog about their experiences and reflect later about what they've done. The online platform is to support people on this powerful journey."

What were their challenges?

"One challenge is always to find meaningful things that people want to talk about online," London said. "Generally, people talk about things online either because it's personal, it's funny, or it's extremely notable."

It also helps to get a celebrity or influential people (like Hugh Jackman) behind you. When another well-known person tweeted about LBL, soon everyone in his sphere knew about it as well.

What's her advice for your organization, if you want to do an online campaign?

- Are you ready to open yourself up? Online dialogue has to be real, not scripted.

- Make it organization-wide: don't designate a solitary person to run "the online campaign." Every staff member has to participate in some way.

- Can you decide on things that are interesting for online discussion?

- You have to be reactive to current affairs.

So, are you ready to dive in?

WHAT THIS BOOK IS...AND ISN'T

At its core, this book is about *philanthropy*. The Greek root of this word weaves *philos* (loving) to *anthropos* (humanity). It's more than a mere feeling. It's action, which is what online giving is about and why you are reading this. We "love" when we nurture, sacrifice for, and enhance—not just when we intend to. Those of us who get married do so with a formal and public vow to love (to do the actions of a loving person regardless of feeling), not to continue merely feeling the love (which would be futile). Sometimes the work we do in charitable spheres can be discouraging (as anything can be), but we press on because of the commitment we have to those we serve.

Whom do we serve?

We serve various kinds of people by meeting their immediate needs (human and social services), helping them realize their potential (through education), or tapping into their deepest desires for beauty, inspiration, and hope (through arts, cultural, and religious institutions). We love others who cannot love themselves because they are disempowered and have no voice. Or perhaps they do have a voice, but still need help being heard. We do that, too! We have a wonderful vocation.

The classic definition of philanthropy dates to President Lyndon Johnson's cabinet member John Gardner, who summed it up as "private initiatives for the public good, focusing on quality of life." This is different in kind and outcome than business, which concerns private initiatives for private good, focusing on material prosperity. Government consists of public initiatives (paid for by public money) for the public good, focusing on law and order. There is balance between them, as well as overlap. But all too often these days, nonprofits are swayed to present themselves as slick businesses. And too often companies present themselves as primarily public do-gooders. Their charitable work is good, but corporations in aggregate contribute about 5% of the roughly $300 billion dollars in total donated each year, and much of their charity work is aimed at increasing their own public awareness to increase profits. And as well they should: that's their role and responsibility to shareholders and employees.

Nonprofits have a distinct and separate niche—some call it the "third sector"—and a balancing effect in our civil society. Philanthropy is the closest of the three by far to the notion of *sharing* that we are taught when we're young. We act voluntarily, not under compulsion, to give something of ours to (often) strangers so that she or he might have a better life. It's that simple.

So that's one big part of what the book is about.

What is it *not* about?

This book goes into detail on certain aspects of online giving that are important to anyone involved in creating an online giving effort or making an online gift. Security is one example, so we provide technical detail on how money moves around after a gift is given. Yet, this book is not about how to build a giving page from a technical standpoint. Web designers and IT professionals will want to consult a good resource on e-commerce and its issues. Secure Sockets Layer and other security features are mentioned occasionally, but this aspect of online giving is not treated exhaustively.

You might notice as you read that there are a lot of examples of giving in the religion sector. However this book is not ideologically driven. The fact is, at least in the United States, that the "religion" sector of charitable giving has been historically the most robust, and you can't open *The Chronicle of Philanthropy* without seeing news about giving in this sector. Also, many larger religious organizations (Salvation Army and World Vision would be good examples) work at such a large scale that their data provides us with good research and conclusions. The assumption behind this book is that we all want to make a difference through our giving and asking others to give, so the goal in writing is to find and explain the very best principles, tools, and case studies to equip you to do that. What happens in each of us as we give (as I outlined earlier based on my own experiences) is the key: this personal transformation is what we want *for* others, and it's what we want to facilitate on a large scale.

This book is also about the private sector's best practices that the nonprofit sector can learn from. The best companies are most certainly "on a mission" of their own, as we are in philanthropy. Reading Steve Jobs's obituary and all the commentary following his death, you can't help but come to that conclusion. If the way businesses get to their markets helps us engage our own constituents in meaningful and sustainable ways, then it's worth studying.

HOW TO USE THIS BOOK

- **One book, two audiences.** In the first section, we want to give the professional fundraiser certain technical information they need to be able to launch a successful online giving program or campaign. But we also want to give the volunteer fundraiser (the one participating in the walk-a- thon, or the new board member of a start-up nonprofit) tools that relate more to being on the outside of an organization. These two audiences work closely together on many charitable efforts, so it makes sense to offer the necessary content in a single book.

- **Redundancies.** You may find redundancies, especially with certain technical information, in various chapters throughout this book. This is intentional. This book is designed to have the necessary information you need in each stand-alone section.

- **Appendices.** There are a few appendices. A chart you will want to refer to while online is seen in Appendix A. It lists the online giving platforms and their functionalities and fees, as well as charity evaluation services and their aspects.

- **"IRL." In Real Life.** Even Mapquest tells us before we print the directions we see online and start driving to "do a reality check." Likewise, I've included in certain chapters some real-life parallels of what we're discussing in principle online. So much of what influences us in real life, especially in our consumer behavior, gets translated into our online experience, that it's helpful to refer back to our offline "real" lives regularly.

TECHNICAL NOMENCLATURE

- An **Interchange fee** is what is imposed on credit card sales and represents a percentage of the sale price paid to credit card companies on every transaction.

- **Secure Sockets Layer,** or **SSL,** encrypts the segments of network connections. Its cousin is the **Transport Layer Security (TLS).** Anytime you have an online financial transaction, one of these is present in the background.[1]

- **Search Engine Optimization (SEO)** is the process of improving the visibility of a website or page in certain unpaid search results.[2]

- **Automated Clearing House (ACH)** is a secure payment transfer network that connects all U.S. financial institutions. Rules governing the network are established by the National Automated Clearing House Association and the Federal Reserve.[3]

- The ACH network acts as the central clearing facility for all **Electronic Fund Transfer (EFT) transactions** that occur nationwide.

---

[1]Source: VeriSign.
[2]Wikipedia has an extensive Notes section and Bibliography on SEO.
[3]Sources: Search Security.

ᔤ1ᖾ

Me? Raise Money?

N͟o one grows up wanting to be a fundraiser.

At least I didn't.

And in nearly two decades of working in this field, I've never met anyone who spent their childhood dreaming of becoming a professional fundraiser, or dressed up as one on Halloween. No child asks their mother to come to class on "Career Day" to talk about her work asking people to consider how a deferred charitable gift annuity can both help the donor in retirement while also providing needed scholarship money for disadvantaged students from economically depressed neighborhoods. *Jeesh, can we please hear from the dad who designs iPad apps?* (My own son wished I directed horror films, so he could tell his friends I have a "cool job.")

Yet here you are. You're raising money either as a professional or as a volunteer. Either you're doing it because you chose to or because someone "put you up to it." You might have done a lot of fundraising for an institution offline and are tasked with raising money online for the first time, or you might have done a little bit of micro-fundraising or crowdsourcing successfully and want to take it to the next level.

This can be one of the most rewarding—or dreadful— experiences you've ever had, depending on how it's executed and depending on your mindset regarding online giving. Remember this: no one likes to *ask* for money, but many people like to *give* money, especially when they feel like doing so creates a solution. Online giving/fundraising (just like offline fundraising) is about creating the right atmosphere for the right people to give to a cause greater than themselves.

Here's what one friend wrote to me when I asked her about her giving practices, which are mostly offline but have lessons about online giving:

> Gifts to my church [result from] duty, gratitude, and obedience. Big gifts ($2,000+) come from family choices. Usually things that our extended family supports. These would be larger annual gifts and capital campaign gifts. We don't evaluate *whether* to give anymore, but rather *how much* and *when*. Sometimes the gift is in stock. It is often a multi-year commitment. The casual gift (<$2,000) may be a special event, or one-time need. This is in

response to a friend asking. We get asked lots. I will give $50–100 away to luncheons and other events that I don't want to attend just to be done with it.

The last line is key.

When you get solicitations to give online, it's incredibly easy to say "no." Right? In fact, it's all too possible that a certain number of those I solicited from my list of 1,200 were making small gifts after the second or third email just to have me "go away."

So what's the secret for making it easy, and even desirable, to give online? And what's the secret to having people stay on your email list and not "UNSUBSCRIBE"?

The key is to engage people with a compelling vision greater than themselves to the point that you're not asking them for money so much as making it easy for them to give to something they believe in—something that inspires them. The key is to create an online community to which you invite these constituents, a community that allows them to take multiple actions—volunteer, share news with friends, give money, or even observe at a distance until they're ready to participate. When organizations want to engage donors online, they need to connect with them first through community because donors don't want organizations using the Internet simply as one more solicitation tool. People who are online are by nature active—they're engaging as they surf the Web—and they are community-oriented (using social media, writing comments on blogs and newspaper articles, sending emails, and instant messaging). They're looking to participate, not to be ordered around. Treat online givers as community partners, build a marketing plan with this assumption, and gifts will flow naturally from the mutual respect that's present.

These next few sections establish certain contexts for you, depending on your experience level and role.

FIRST TIMER?

You're trying to raise money for the first time online—either as a professional or a volunteer. Maybe you're even raising money for the first time, period.

For now, imagine you're in your favorite coffee shop. There are people talking with friends and others who are waiting in line by themselves. There are people at tables socializing and others working on their laptops or typing away furiously on smartphones. You spot the ones on phones around the shop and might think, "Social media really takes people out of the moment."

Now, it's true: social media removes people from those standing around them. And yes, there are people squirreled away at home or office late at night using social media instead of playing with the kids, visiting with their spouses, or completing their overtime work. But the vast majority of those on social media platforms are engaging with friends—usually fairly tight circles—through Facebook or Twitter or scores of other social media platforms, or texting, which is a social media channel in itself. My twelve-year-old son is getting more and more group text messages, which my wife and I review regularly.

Further imagine an individual cloud above each person on a smartphone with groups of people like them all talking to each other. Some of these clouds in your favorite coffee shop are in fact overlapping even though the people standing there don't realize it. They are "in their own world," but they are also in their own "moments," fully engaged, discussing what's important to them.

Suddenly, one of these people gets an alert from an iPhone app letting her know that there's been a 7.1 magnitude earthquake in Haiti. Thousands, perhaps tens of thousands, are feared dead (We learn later the death toll is 220,000).

OMG, she texts to her friend, *did u hear about the haiti quake?*

She and her friend text back and forth, and in a few minutes she learns of a way to make a donation to help. She decides to donate $10—the maximum allowed via text—and since it goes on her phone bill, it's easy to decide on. In the days following, more than three million people do just what she did.

While this is more accurately called "mobile giving," it's a form of electronic giving and also a demonstration of the power of a strong community that is motivated to solve a problem.

When the Haiti earthquake hit in January 2010, it revolutionized the power of those little clouds you're imagining right now. As documented by CharityVillage.com, tens of thousands of mobile device users—given a 5-digit code through news sources covering the disaster as well as charities like the Red Cross—sent a text message and thereby donated $5 or $10 to help with relief efforts. The Mobile Giving Foundation said that after less than four weeks, more than U.S. $35 million had been collected through these texts. More than that, the foundation said that at one point they were getting "10,000 text messages a second." The American Red Cross alone received $32 million from more than three million people making $10 donations.[4]

This money was used for emergency shelters, clean water, medical attention, and eventually to rebuild schools and buildings destroyed or damaged. But were it not for immediate giving tools—and the ability to reach people online and on their mobile devices—the call for help would be delayed and the cash would be tied up or spent on something else. It's not an exaggeration to say that donations made by texts saved thousands of lives in Haiti.

If you're new to online giving, I'd like you to try something. Go to the page for the American Red Cross (just to pick one that almost everyone knows) and read what it says about text giving. If you want to try it out, go for it. Right now, the limit is $10 for these kinds of donations, and they usually show up on your phone bill. You won't get a separate receipt from the charity. But I'd like to ask you to try making a text gift *today*, whether it's the Red Cross or something else. Of, if you feel more comfortable, make a first-time gift online at the Red Cross or some other charity. It's easy and fun and will make you feel good. And, as you can see above, you can do significant good when you combine forces with others.

YES, I CAN SPELL CROWDSOURCE (FOR THE EXPERIENCED ONLINE USER)

Perhaps you've already done a fair amount of fundraising. If so, this book will help you take that knowledge to the next

---

[4]Source: Convio. Online marketing benchmark study, March 2011.

level. Appendix A will come in handy, allowing you to survey the landscape of online giving platforms. Appendix B will help you know how to evaluate those charities you already support and the ones you're considering supporting.

If you're not already on various social media platforms (Facebook, Twitter, YouTube), you will want to consider doing so or ramping up your involvement prior to your next online effort. These platforms will help you leverage your efforts. Appendix A lists the online giving tools that incorporate various social media.

For you, the next evolution in your online philanthropy may well be to supplement it with offline activity. An increasing number of people who are getting engaged with causes online—in particular clean water, orphans, human trafficking, disaster relief—are going offline, taking trips to the places they've only visited in photos and videos, and then photoblogging or videoblogging to build community and raise funds.

FOR THE PROFESSIONAL

Whether you're a development assistant, VP for advancement, or executive director of a small nonprofit and you have to do it all, this book will serve as a compendium of the best resources available.

Let's first look at some quick stats, available as of the end of 2011[5]:

---

[5]Sources: Convio, Blackbaud, Giving USA, Chronicle of Philanthropy, M+R Strategic Services.

- Growth of online giving in dollars from 2009 to 2010: 14%

- Growth in number of online gifts from 2009 to 2010: 7%

- Median gift online in 2010: $92

- Median gift online in 2009: $83

- Largest online gift reported in 2010: $100,000

- Percentage of total giving constituted by online giving (in tracked charities): 7%

- Median growth in number of email addresses for charities tracked: 22%

Your website in general is vital to healthy online and offline giving. Convio, an Austin-based company providing customized "social fundraising" solutions, found that 49% of mid-level and major donors will visit a charity's website before making a first-time gift online or through the mail.

The professional fundraiser will want to get ahold of white papers by Convio, as well as industry peers Blackbaud and M+R Strategic Services. Fundraising consultancies such as Sage, The Bridgespan Group, and CompassPoint Nonprofit Consulting also have good white papers.

One finding in the M+R report[6] is that some charitable sectors, such as "Environmental" and "Rights" organizations (to use M+R categories), get more online gifts through email than do

---

[6]http://www.e-benchmarksstudy.com/

other sectors, such as "Health," "International" or "Wildlife/Animal Welfare." On average, charities get 43% of their online gifts through email marketing efforts. The former two sectors met or beat that percentage. The other sectors found that most of their online gifts came not through organization-driven email marketing, but rather through peer-to-peer emails and grassroots efforts.

REALITY CHECK ON ONLINE GIVING

On Mashable, the website covering digital culture, writer Sarah Kessler in an early 2011 post[7] underscored what is a key principle of this book: "Most nonprofits who successfully use social media," she wrote, "see it as a tool to engage donors rather than make transactions." Others have called the Internet a strategic marketing tool.

This also affirms the M+R report data referred to previously. That is, most online donations don't come as a result of emails sent by the organization to the donor. (That approach is rapidly becoming like direct mail in its look and feel and the saturation of charities using it. Anyone using MailChimp, Constant Contact, WorldMerge, or another email distribution program can watch open and click-through rates drop over time.) Rather, most online gifts (57%) emerge from relationships built online between organization and donor and even between existing donor and new donor (friend/peer). Charities that raise money successfully and sustainably online are the ones that approach the Internet as a relationship-building

---

[7]Source: Mashable. "5 Facebook Giving Campaign Success Stories," January 17, 2011. http://mashable.com/2011/01/17/facebook-giving/

town square attracting citizens to a "commons" rather than as a hunter's rifle selecting targets.

Wise nonprofits also understand that many first-time givers to your organization will have taken a look at your group online and then made a gift, regardless of whether that gift comes online or through the mail (see Wired Wealthy Study, co-authored by Convio in 2008). This is true for older givers, who are doing due diligence, as well as younger donors, who are looking to see whether your mission aligns with their priorities. It's not hard to understand that if busy donors are doing due diligence using one of the watchdog groups online (GuideStar, Charity Navigator, and others), they'll simply navigate over to your charity's website. The watchdog groups list the website URL along with the IRS Form 990 (as on GuideStar) and other information.

Online giving logically only stands to increase because of the technological nature of our society and the increased significance of computers in our daily lives. Some charity leaders believe mobile giving and volunteering may eclipse online giving (for more on these trends, see some of the innovative efforts by DoSomething.org).

Younger generations will increasingly look to the Web to evaluate your charity. To neglect an online strategy is to neglect the table at which younger donors are sitting.

Four of the five successful campaigns that Kessler profiled in her Mashable post promoted event- or time-oriented initiatives to raise money. They built in a sense of urgency to raising money. In both 2009 and 2010, special event fundraising (live events) was a booming business. People rally to once-only opportunities, and the more your organization can sponsor a do-it-now way to engage givers, the more donation income will be realized.

The non-event-specific online campaign profiled by Kessler—Timberland's Earthkeeper app—made micro-events out of users' tendencies to use the app in their spare time. The campaign meets users where they already are. This trend has even become a new effort among musicians and others. A site called Downtime[8] allows traveling musicians, athletes, and actors to use their spare time to do something charitably, whether it's simply tweet out a link they see or direct their fans to do something for an organization they care about. This builds their fan loyalty and also extends the reach of the charity.

These are all very exciting prospects for the future, but currently online giving is not a significant portion of a nonprofit's donation revenue pie. Even the American Red Cross, which raises about a third of its $3.5 billion budget in private support, took in only 16% of its gifts online during 2010, including the tremendous outpouring of support via text and online for Haiti earthquake relief. Normally, the percentage of online giving is in the low single digits. World Vision, with almost all its budget coming through private support and with very successful child sponsorship and disaster response and relief programs, still only takes in about 3.5% of its total giving online.

Yet, small as it is compared with major gifts, foundation grants and (for some) direct mail, online giving is becoming more and more of an entry point for first-time givers and this

---

[8]Find it at: http://mydowntime.com/wordpress/

will only increase in proportion as younger donors get older and seek ways to engage with the world around them. The Internet allows your organization to welcome potential new givers and volunteers with a common table to facilitate conversation and, yes, occasionally to ask for help. What the Internet is *not* is a door to their house or apartment.

Just as it's important to understand the place of online giving in the total revenue pie—for us fundraising professionals—we cannot view online giving as one separate effort among others. At its core, online giving flows from online community. The non-professionals reading this book know this. They know the Internet is the glue that holds all of a charity's efforts in place, and that "online giving" itself is somewhat of a misnomer. It's probably more accurate to talk about "fast" giving (online) and "slow" giving (mail). And don't forget "impulse" giving—the smartphone.

Let's take an extreme example to illustrate.

Convio[9] says that nonprofits should view the Internet as a "strategic marketing tool." Before President Obama's off-the-chart online fundraising success in 2008, there was Howard Dean in 2004. Governor Dean at one point had more than two thousand micro-fundraisers ("Dean Team" leaders), who between their efforts and others raised $3.6 million online, nearly half of the $7.5 million total raised by the campaign.

While it's true that organizations must plan prudently around online giving versus more traditional methods of seeking

---

[9]Source: http://events.convio.com/site/News2?page=NewsArticle&id=2600624

support, it's also true that an informed understanding of online community and social media behavior can exponentially increase a charity's online support. The direct and indirect benefits stem from viewing the Internet as a way to engage existing constituents and attract new constituents in a community that's unified by a single vision.

Therefore, online giving is not a budget savior but rather a community builder. It's tempting for those of us who have the pressures of meeting an operating budget to think that if we just put something on the Internet, where there are billions of people, we'll certainly raise enough to make that 10% shortfall in the next three weeks before the fiscal year closes. Or that the immediacy of reaching our core constituency online will prompt them to give. Or, we think that we should start our campaign off with a bang and announce it online as soon as we have our message finalized. *Don't do it!* This, again, is like treating online giving as though it were direct mail, and that the Internet is the door to where the donor lives.

The good news is that of 430 nonprofits studied in 2010 by Convio, 79% raised more online year-over-year, while only 21% experienced declines. (Much of this depends on which category you're in—education, healthcare, international affairs, and so on. And, if indeed your organization is in the international relief sector and you don't already have a well-oiled online and mobile giving functionality to your development operation … put this book down now and contact the Mobile Giving Foundation.)

Assuming, though, that you're not in international relief, and if you're comfortable with the 1% to 3% that online gifts can provide, what they do also—and do best—is identify potential major donors as well as build community.

So we return to the question of "why?" Why was I willing to email all 1,200 of my contacts? Why are you asking friends for $25 and $50 gifts so you can spend a Saturday afternoon walking 15 or 26 or 35 miles?

You might be making a gift after hearing a two-line story like, "my mother died of breast cancer, and I'm walking in the Avon Walk next month. Would you sponsor me for $50?" Or even a 160-character text on your phone like, " 'Injustice anywhere is a threat to justice everywhere.' –MLK Jr. Fight injustice. Donate canned food for those in need. Txt HUNGER."[10] The story might have been much longer. An article, blog post, or a link at the end of a Kindle edition book that inspired you. Without the story, there's no vision for what was, is, and what could be. A story, and especially a good one, can completely engage the giver.

Through charitable giving online, a united community creates and embodies change for the common good. And if we want to make a difference in the twenty-first century, we have to use the latest technology to our advantage, and we have to collaborate as a global community.

---

[10]Actual text from DoSomething.org.

2

Where Does The Money Go?

Making purchases online has become so second nature to us that we often fail to realize that we don't really know *where the money goes* once we click "confirm." We think about it now and then when we hear about identity theft, or when we are asked to update our credit card information on the sites we visit the most. But we don't really know what happens behind the curtains of online gift and product transactions.

SHOPPING'S AS EASY AS ONE CLICK

Online security is a huge issue. But first, we need to study how we behave online—how we navigate and shop—because this determines so much about how we give online.

In 1999, Amazon received a United States patent for its "1-Click" ordering system (this patent was contested and then was confirmed in early 2010[11]). In 2000, Amazon licensed it to Apple for its online store. Apple later added it to iTunes.

It's no wonder why shopping on Amazon (or Apple) is so fun. And so common. It's easy. Who wouldn't want to get the product they want immediately? No lines, no credit card swipe (you already established your account the first time you made a purchase or created an Apple ID), no waiting on the credit card slip to print out and sign. These are the design details that affect our lives. In the industrialized world we live with time-saving choices. Which option saves us more seconds? Forget about days, hours, and minutes. No one has time like that anymore. We deal in seconds.

Online giving lives in this fast-paced world.

Amazon has done something else now. It's the Amazon Wish List Browser Button for your toolbar. Install it, and when you're on sites other than Amazon, you can click on things you want and keep track of items you're interested in to later

---

[11]The Sydney Morning Herald (May 23, 2006) chronicled the beginning of the U.S. Patent Office reexamination of Apple's patent.

purchase back on Amazon's website. "Everything+." I added this toolbar feature to Firefox. After a 20-second installation and restart, I navigated over to Etsy, because that site was one of the options on the Wish List orientation page that Firefox took me to after installation (it's also one of my wife's favorites, so I need to be familiar with it). The first thing I see on Etsy is a 1.5-inch thick screen header explaining how to add an item to my Amazon wish list. (That is, how not to order that item off the Etsy site then and there, in other words. In fact, Amazon got slammed in late 2011 by Senator Olympia Snowe and others for its "Price-Check" app that allows customers in stores to scan the bar codes or QR codes of products, check Amazon's inventory, and get a 5% discount to buy off Amazon.[12]) Just for fun, I navigate to Barnes & Noble to see if the Wish List works there—on the competitor's site who tried to institute "Express Lane" but was sued by Amazon and now has nearly-as-good two-click ordering. Of course, Amazon will add items from BN.com to my wish list. Anything to accommodate me, the buyer, who likes mainly to walk around B&N but shop online.

One more thing worth noting about the Wish List tool. Amazon held a ten-week long promotion at the end of 2011. When you added an item from another site you were automatically entered into a sweepstakes each week to win a Amazon gift card worth $2,500. This incentivizing even the smallest task online has been carefully noted by charity officials, who know it's more and more of a challenge to ask someone to do something for "free."

---

[12]Bloomberg News. December 9, 2011. http://www.bloomberg.com/news/2011-12-09/snowe-asks-amazon-to-halt-price-check-promo.html

Here are some take-aways from Amazon and its Wish List button:

- **Easy even for a couch potato.** How can one click on the Internet be any easier? It's like the point-and-shoot camera was to photography.

- **The company goes where you are.** Any company that lasts knows that it has to go where the customers are and sell to them the way they want to be sold to.

- **You are "fair game."** Just because you buy from other stores doesn't mean Amazon won't come into those stores with you—perhaps riding the plastic saddle of that smartphone—and try to entice you to buy from them. This is not a do-as-if lesson necessarily for charities, but you have to admire how relentless and innovative they've been in order to pursue their mission.

- **Location, Location, Location.** The three things a retail company knows it's all about, after all. Likewise, in the twenty-first century, Web domains are the new real estate, and smart nonprofits know that they either have to drive traffic to their real estate—an increasingly challenging task that has spawned the new alphabet soup concept SEO— or they, like Amazon, have to find where people are and go to them. There is a legend that a pair of Christian missionaries was hiking up the tallest populated peak in Nepal in the mid-1900s to share the good news, and on the way up they saw a Coca-Cola salesman headed down, his case empty. When you're passionate about what you do, you find a way to get to your customer. And before the other guy does.

Some charities are using this same go-where-the-customer-is approach and have co-branded with companies to "round-up for charity." The Company Change Round-Up[13] boasts "donation attach rates" of 70%[14] (meaning that 70% of the people seeing the option to donate choose it). Consider talking to local businesses or your vendors to see if they'll consider using this tool. Does your local Staples have a program like this in place? Perhaps they should, for your organization and others. Having real estate located in the transaction window, where buyers are asked to make a relatively small increase in what they are already planning to spend, is an unbeatable advantage.

- **Make it fun.** The Wish List button to the left of the URL nav bar, the "a" and its friendly smile include a small, provocative blue "+" dimple on the smile. You can't help but click on it to see if the item you want is listed on Amazon. Not since many of us filled out a wedding registry have we given in to the indulgence of navigating a store, pointing out the things we want.

- **Embody trust.** Amazon is a trusted site. Even people who sell through Amazon are trusted by virtue of association. What Amazon presents as much as a global inventory is the message of, "If you see it, we'll beat anyone's price on it, and we'll get it to you overnight. Trust us."

Amazon's big weakness, though, is a charity's strength. I'm guessing you've used Amazon. And I'm guessing most people you know have used it. But do you feel that using that

---

[13] Change Round-Up

[14] Change Round-Up cites blog by "Oldest Living Digital Marketer Tells All." http://www.oldestliving.com/2008/09/change-round-up-proof-positive-that.html

site and even commenting on it about the books you've read places you in an "Amazon community"? I don't feel substantially any more connected to book lovers who shop or comment on Amazon.com than I do to Big Mac fans eating at McDonalds. We're all there to consume the greasy flat thing and then get back in our cars to drive off. Amazon's purpose is for us to go there *to shop*, not to create community. It's one reason Barnes & Noble got in financial trouble: too much community and not enough buying. (There was a five-story Barnes & Noble near Lincoln Center in New York City, and many of us would run into friends there and chat, or read and have naps in comfortable chairs. But we wouldn't buy much and thereby support the business, and the location is now a Century 21, with fewer places to sit down.)

Shopping online is largely an individual experience. This is your strength as a charity: to buck the trends of retail and to create a community where people come together, putting aside purely personal agendas, and do something for the community they're a part of, or for some community halfway around the world. Sounds corny, but it's true. The missionaries going to Nepal knew the power of community. They were sent by a strong community, they were traveling in community, and they were trying to establish a community. Their failure, however, was in not walking quickly enough. It's hard to beat retailers at their own game, so you may want to find partnership opportunities with businesses and others.

SECURITY AND ONLINE FINANCIAL TRANSACTIONS FOR THE INTERNET-LEERY

Online consumer behavior varies in many ways from online philanthropic behavior, but security issues are very significant issues in both cases, so let's look at where our money actually goes; that is, what happens when we click "submit." Though many of us are accustomed to making online financial transactions, it's always good to be able to answer questions donors have about security and efficiency.

So how can you be sure the technology of the Internet will not dump your checking account into a charity's bank account by accident? Or, more likely, how can you ensure hackers can't get into your transactions?

Secure Sockets Layer, or SSL, encrypts the segments of network connections. Its cousin is the Transport Layer Security (TLS). They are similar, but they do not interoperate. Anytime you make an online financial transaction, one of these is running in the background.[15] Different versions of each operate in basic Internet-based applications such as web browsing, email, and instant messaging, and also with Internet faxing and Voice-over Internet Protocol (VoIP). Essentially, TLS and SSL operate so that client/server applications can communicate with each other without anyone else eavesdropping on or tampering with that communication. To avoid digressing into a discussion on programming, suffice it to say you should check with an IT professional about this, and also ask whether you'd be using TLS or SSL. Some groups, like The National Institute of Standards and Technology, rate the older versions of TLS as more desirable than the newer versions of SSL for a number of reason[16] (Gmail uses TLS v1.0).

---

[15]Source: VeriSign.

[16]National Institute of Standards and Technology (December 2010). "Implementation Guidance for FIPS PUB 140-2 and the Cryptographic Module Validation Program".

So, beyond "is it safe?" we need to now ask, what happens once I click "submit"?

For starters, and to find out how online financial transactions actually work, you can find a diagrammatic overview at Idealware.org.[17]

The transaction includes four elements:

• The website (what the donor sees)

• Fraud control

• A merchant account

• The charity's bank account

The Website. Whether it's the charity's own website, or third-party web tool that the charity can put its brand on to accept and process gifts, this is the element that donors see. It's the storefront and the sales floor itself. This element might comprise the donor's navigation to the donation page, filling in contact and payment information (if it's a first-time gift), and clicking on "confirm," all on three or more subsequent screens. Or, it might be a much quicker process similar to Amazon or iTunes (Ticket Cake, for instance, modeled their ease-of-use after iTunes).

VERY IMPORTANT: One charity I know inadvertently designed its giving page so that the final step in the transaction—the one where people click "confirm"—was positioned below

---

[17]http://www.idealware.org/articles/payment_processing_pictures.php

the screen's lower margin, meaning you had to scroll down to confirm. So donors would "Enter Gift" on the penultimate screen and, led to the next where they didn't see any actions called for, never realize they hadn't confirmed it. *Make sure* to position your final confirmation in the middle of the web page or clearly in view of the user. Certainly, a "progress bar" at the top of the screen (if you need more than three pages to process a gift) is advisable, and a simple confirmation message ("Thank you for your gift!") will minimize lost gifts due to poor page layout. A graduate school paper by Heidi Adkisson (found on her website[18]) has helpful tips on standards to use.

Fraud Control. I hope hearing about the next element will assure many newcomers to this field. If you always wanted to grow up to be a fraud control expert—though why you wouldn't choose fundraiser over fraud control is beyond me—you can simply go to BestPaymentGateways.com and read more on this subject.

Essentially, fraud control relies on something called a "payment gateway," which facilitates electronic transactions.

Here's the process in a nutshell:

- The customer makes a purchase online.

- The Internet browser being operated by the customer uses SSL or TSL encryption to "scramble" the information being sent.

---

[18] http://www.hpadkisson.com/index.html

- The charity's website takes the donor's credit card details and forwards them to the "payment gateway." The payment gateway is separately hosted in some cases, and encryption is still necessary.

- The payment gateway takes the information and sends the details to the bank used by the business (This is one entity beyond the merchant account, which is element #3 and described below).

- The bank sends the request to the card association. In the case of American Express or Discover, the card association serves as the bank, and a response can then be issued. If the card used has a MasterCard or Visa logo, additional steps occur.

- With Visa or MasterCard, the card association forwards the information to the bank that issued the card. This is the customer's bank.

- The customer's bank assesses whether or not there are sufficient funds to cover the transaction.

- The issuing bank then sends an authorization code to the payment processor card association on whether or not to allow the transaction to go through. The authorization code corresponds to the reason for a decline if there is one, or simply includes the code that allows the transaction to take place.

- The payment processor sends the authorization code to the payment gateway.

- The payment gateway then sends the code on to the charity. If the transaction is declined, the gift process is terminated.

If the transaction is approved, the gift goes through and the money is placed on "hold" from the customer's account in a merchant account (covered next).

This all takes between two and ten seconds, depending on connection speed and site traffic.

Merchant Account. Once the payment gateway approves the gift transaction, the money goes from the bank into a "merchant account." If a Visa or MC is used, then it might be Chase Visa or US Airways MC, for instance, that is sending the money to the account. American Express and Discover serve as their own banks and send the user's money to merchant accounts. A merchant account's sole purpose is to hold credit card payments. If you're a charity and want to start receiving online gifts, you have to establish a merchant account or find a vendor with one already, like PayPal.

Bank account. Your charity's bank account will not receive the money from the merchant account right away. Typically, merchant accounts hold payments two to three days. If you use a merchant account belonging to a vendor (like PayPal) you would expect payments once or twice per month. Nevertheless, the charity can usually see the payments in real time and can also receipt donors for their gifts right away.

Online auctions or raffles, because of their nature and sometimes the nature of organizations or payers using them, sometimes require "high-risk credit card processing." Under this classification of online transaction, auctions and raffles get treated the same as payments to gun dealers, pawn shops, and bail bondsmen (if only my eleven-year-old son knew his father ran with such a tough crowd...). You should check with your vendor and outline all the potential functionalities of your online giving program to make sure that your online activity isn't classified in a way that requires this processing. To keep it simple, consider using an online auction site like CharityBuzz.

To reiterate another option, instead of giving online via credit card, you can also offer Automated Clearing House (ACH) or Electronic Fund Transfer (EFT) giving functionalities. (These are considered the same but are instead closely similar, and there are slight differences including cost. Check with your bank.) These are increasing in popularity, and more than $19 trillion in transactions were conducted in 2010, an increase of 3% over from 2009, according to *Treasury & Risk*'s e-newsletter. This option involves the same security features of credit card giving, of course, but avoids the fees of merchant accounts and processing. Often, there's a bank charge for each transaction, but it is fixed and is usually more efficient for gifts of any significant size (e.g., $20 or more).

For nonprofit professionals, at this point it's worth touching on three issues charities should ask themselves about credit cards. They are philosophical in nature and easily dismissible (we fundraisers are practical folk, no?), but as this book discusses how philanthropy comes out of and contributes to strong communities, they're relevant issues. Donors as well may want to read this so they can ask their favorite charity's development director about it.

The first is about the unintended effects of credit card use. There are two groups of people who are directly and negatively impacted by credit card use: small business owners (and charities), and lower income individuals and families.

The Federal Reserve Bank of Boston published a paper[19] in the summer of 2010 which pointed out that most merchants set the same price for goods no matter whether someone is paying by cash or credit. This is not news. So what's the problem? The first group getting hurt by credit cards are merchants (and charities), who pay an "interchange fee" on credit card sales (a percentage of the sale price paid to credit card companies on every transaction; we'll cover the details and amounts of the fee in Chapter 3, Section "One Word: Plastic"). Usually the percentage is fixed at around 2%, but as the price of the good goes up, so of course does the interchange fee. For instance, you might have seen gas stations charging one price for cash and one for credit cards. For them, $2.50 in cash is better by 2% than $2.50 with your Visa card at the pump. But when gas rose closer to $4.00 per gallon, some small business owners stopped taking credit cards.[20] Interchange fees, debit card swipe fees and discounts, and caps on both are all in play in Congress and by the Federal Reserve, so if you're a charity official, watch the legislation coming out since the Dodd-Frank Act and its impact on credit and debit card use.

---

[19]"Who Gains and Who Loses from Credit Card Payments: Theory and Calibrations." FRB/Boston. Site here: http://www.bos.frb.org/economic/ppdp/2010/ppdp1003.htm. Also covered in the July 27, 2010 online edition of The Wall Street Journal.

[20]Some merchants have switched to using a card by Revolution with a lower interchange fee: http://www.revolutioncard.com/ Included are some large retailers, such as Walgreens, Office Depot and GameStop. I am not aware of charities that accept the Revolution card for online gifts.

There's a second group that can feel the pinch of your credit card use, albeit indirectly. Poor families and individuals who pay for goods in cash actually pay more for that milk and bread than you do, since the prices merchants establish include their costs of paying the interchange fee that is incurred by your credit card use. Besides, you'll benefit from credit card rewards, cash-back, miles, etc. Certainly, food stamps mitigate the lack of parity, and we're talking about charitable giving rather than buying groceries. Yet, when we go online, giving becomes such a quick and simple and—yes, mindless—action on our part that to use our credit cards to make charitable gifts as commonly as we buy groceries does have a negative side effect on the charity. It's preferable to look into ACH transfers or EFT, even though it will take you more time to set up through your online bank account. As the chart in Appendix A will show, some online giving platforms (the kind micro-fundraisers might use for smaller nonprofits) don't accommodate recurring gifts, so EFTs are sometimes the only option for you to give automatically on a monthly or periodic basis.

As much fault as I find with credit cards, however, they can still be a great tool for donors and charities. And if the credit card gift is an automatic monthly charge, the overall benefits may outweigh the fees.

One example of a charity that encourages givers to move away from credit card giving is a church where my friend is the minister. They inform parishioners of their options (which includes credit cards) but also tell them about the fees.[21]

---

[21]To check out the language they use on their site, go to Restoration Anglican Church in Arlington, VA.

They let them know that they can use plastic but the church will be charged 3%⁺ (depending on the card), or they can set up an ACH transfer for $0.45 per transaction. If your gift is $15 or more, your transaction is costing the charity more money than necessary. There's a couple in Houston who routinely makes six-figure gifts online, though this is the exception. They rack up the airline miles, but the charity leaves a percentage of that gift on the table. Imagine if all your largest gifts had interchange fees, even if those fees were capped! Though gifts of this size are rare, the charity software company Blackbaud found that 88% of more than 1,800 organizations it tracks received at least one $1,000 gift online per year. Consider the scale of all those mid-range gifts and the interchange fees that your charity might be losing. Setting up an ACH transfer online by typing in checking account information and adding the routing and account number can be accomplished in a minute or two, even though it can be a hassle, and the donor can even instruct the bank to send a recurring gift immediately following a paycheck deposit. It can make a real difference for the charity at the end of the year.

This begs our second question. Does losing 3% to 4.5% of a gift's value through merchant and credit card company fees, along with other processing fees below, justify your accepting credit cards to begin with? While for small businesses this can be a real issue, for most charities it's almost a non-starter. The interchange fees retailers pay cut into profits, which are not at stake when donors make a charitable gift. It merely lessens the overall value of a gift. One way to lessen the negative impact: consider asking donors who use credit cards to donate their miles or card rewards to those whom your charity serves, or to pledge their year-end cash-back to your charity.

Finally, how much are you encouraging your donors to take on debt? Are you encouraging them to be charitable, versus giving in order to get tangible benefits? I encourage you to have discussions during your nonprofit leadership meetings about how much you promote credit card giving versus bank transfers, especially among younger donors trying to avoid taking on too much debt. And if you're a donor, please consider how much you give via credit card versus in cash or stock and what that's costing the charity in lost donation revenue. (Stock is the smartest way to give anyway, since you'll avoid capital gains tax if it's appreciated and you've had it a year or longer.)

These three questions, admittedly, are a bit "sermonesque." (I did once want to be a minister. And a baseball player and an astronomer.)

Katya Andreson, in Robin Hood Marketing, takes the opinion that charities should avoid trying to win donors to "their causes" on the charities' terms and instead view their organizations as entities to be marketed to the donor on the donor's terms and for the donor's benefit. If we take this view to its extreme, we expedite the philanthropic process and we use all tools at our disposal, whether they are credit cards or marketing techniques (and budgets) or heat-map eye-scanning tools on our nonprofit websites. Concerning ourselves with issues like those above might seem tangential to some readers.

While there are some laudable parts to Andreson's argument, and while I wouldn't advocate that the professionals reading this take the tone I sometimes do in persuasion—we're having an "in-house" discussion in this book!—I do believe that the "independent" or "third" sector in America is different from the private and public sectors. We have different "rules" and mores than the private sector has, and nonprofit work dates back to the early 17th century, with the founding of a Massachusetts college through an estate gift by John Harvard and a fundraising trip to England. Professional fundraisers should be as much aware of what's good for a donor and our community as for his or her charity. For without informed donors who are viewed as charity partners and not simply ATMs, there is no sustainable revenue base. Consider givers as you would "old growth forests." OK. Sermon done!

No discussion about credit cards, payment gateways, and financial transactions would be complete, though, without a look into the offline world of retail and merchandising. It is merchandising that so informs the way we interact online, for the layout of a page—its simplicity and, frankly, its beauty or its hideousness—will convince us within seconds to remain or navigate away.

IRL (In Real Life): How and why do buyers buy? What consumer behavior can tell us about online charitable giving.

In a survey[22] among active donors and consumers, respondents were asked to describe their favorite retail shopping experiences. Women listed Anthropologie as their #1 choice (followed by Barnes & Noble and Sephora); men listed the Apple Store (followed by Best Buy and Barnes & Noble). We also asked what online retailers people used the most: across the board, Amazon was far-and-away the most used. iTunes was

---

[22]By the author; Fall 2011; email survey sent to 401 recipients; 34% response rate. Recipients were largely urban professionals, 35–55 years old.

a distant second but was valued among a number of respondents. Many respondents indicated making online purchases from retailers who are known for strong in-store experiences: Pottery Barn, Gap Kids, Bed Bath & Beyond, and Apple, to name a few.

When you're in a store and find the experience pleasurable, that's no accident. And when you feel that walking around the store is leisurely, this too is no accident. It's been choreographed and planned and studied. Most of you know this. What you may not know is the term that visual merchandisers refer to in what to avoid in maximizing the shopping (and buying) experience: "excessive disruption." The quick way to say this is: if you make it easy for people to buy, they'll buy. The corollary is that if there are too many onerous steps in the purchasing process or in the look and feel of it, people will turn away before taking that final step of clicking "Confirm."

For many, Apple is the gold standard. As with many things we see now, there is an "Apple" effect on online donation design. Do you know why so many giving websites use rectangles with rounded corners for their SUBMIT buttons? It's because Steve Jobs knew we'd be enamored of them.

Someone said not long ago that good web design itself was no longer a luxury (for a nonprofit as well as a company); rather, it was "the price of entry." A senior Apple official discussed on Gary Hustwit's 2009 documentary "Objectified" how good design made you feel as though, "But of *course* it has to look like that! How could it be any other way?" The logic, the precision, the beauty, the ease, and the peace of mind it gives you; all of these things bestow success upon an object, a place, and even a website.

Apple has been brilliant at eliminating excessive disruption, online and off. I was at the Apple Retail Store in the La

Cantera Mall in San Antonio (the only mall I'll gladly accompany my wife to since I'm able to read outside in rattan armchairs under canopies and mist sprayed into the Texas heat). I had picked out a new pair of earbuds, and an Apple employee saw me looking around for the cashier.[23] She walked over to me and asked if I wanted to check out. I said yes, so she took out an iPhone with a credit card scanner and swiped my card along the side. She asked me if I wanted my receipt emailed to the email address on file (under my Apple ID). I said yes and thanked her, she smiled, and I walked out. It was a Shopping-Averse-Male's dream, and in moments I was back in the rattan chair under the canopy and mist. I had never thought that an excessive disruption might be the time it took to walk over to the cashier, or the "long" line of maybe two or three customers ahead of me.

The parallel for nonprofits isn't hard to imagine. Were a potential donor to be browsing your website for child sponsorship and accosted by random pop-up windows asking her to donate unrelated to her reason for being there, she'd quickly navigate away. I *wanted* to find a cashier at Apple, and their cashier came to me to conduct a seconds-long transaction. No excessive disruption there.

Top designers today talk about the need to cut away everything that's unnecessary from the object itself. Cut, cut, and cut again. Leave only what's necessary. Years ago, when online giving was still relatively new, I did a study for my employer on the

---

[23]The New York Times also profiles Apple's "spot-the-shopper" app. Shoppers can download an app and, once they've shopped online for a product and entered a retail store to pick it up, an Apple employee receives an alert on their device and takes the product over to the shopper. November 25, 2011. http://bits.blogs.nytimes.com/2011/11/25/a-look-at-apples-spot-the-shopper-technology/

top-of-class nonprofits that were raising money online. At the time, the organization raising the most money (3% of its annual budget) was a small Rhode Island child sponsorship group. What they had for a website was a white screen, a photo of a child in the middle, and the words DONATE NOW. That was pretty much it. They raised a lot of money.

To take this a step further and draw some lessons from Apple in relation to your website, online giving, and your donors, I'm going to disappoint you: you're going to have to wait until Chapter 5. The reason is that the answer has a lot to do with beauty, community, and sustainability,

things we haven't covered yet. You might be surprised to learn that Apple is not, in my opinion, the exemplar of what a nonprofit should strive for if it wants to raise money online. For a business, it's top of the class. But in engaging others to sacrifice part of their treasures for someone else, I look at a different organization. It's a nonprofit that exists as much in theory as it does in practice, whose website most of us use each week and sometimes multiple times a day, and which is almost as unglam as it gets. Yet its results— both in fundraising and the community they create—are off the charts.

AFTER THE MONEY'S RECEIVED: HOW TO SAY THANK YOU

Clean water champion charity: water celebrated its fifth birthday this year by sending thank-you videos to supporters who had helped them through the "mycharity: water" campaign, an effort where people "give up their birthday presents" and ask their friends and families to donate to the charity instead. These videos were brief—a little more than a minute.

They starred staff, whose minor mistakes weren't edited out. And they were posted on YouTube.

Which one of us getting one of these would not pass it along to friends and family and say, "Check it out! charity: water did a video for me!" Aside from the sincere goodwill and gratitude the nonprofit used, and the soft and hard costs they incurred making the videos, they were smart. What better way to get their word out than to give supporters a completely non-threatening tool to share with others and potentially introduce new friends to the charity? The page views of the various videos ranges from 59 to 3,461, with those on camera ranging from junior staff members to founder Scott Harrison thanking six-year-old "Mackenzie," who was raising $300 to help fifteen people get water.

The video with 3,461 views went out to the "Glamberts," fans of Adam Lambert, who gave more than $300,000 through nearly 6,000 donations. After initial thanks from two staff members, the director of charity: water's digital engagement came on screen having donned Lambert-like make-up. It was funny, full of camaraderie, and sincere.

The numbers for this campaign so far are quite impressive:

- Nearly 98,000 members

- 171,000 donations

- $13 million raised

- 650,000 people served with clean and safe drinking water

To be able to count the people served, to thank supporters and volunteers with personal and lighthearted videos, and to do it all beautifully, is an effort bound to build on itself.

Another aspect of charity: water's work to note is how they use corporate marketing and technology. They use the best of videography, writing, and emails and don't flinch from making their presentation stand up next to a Fortune 500 company's online—even though they're funded through public support—but what they call people to is self-sacrifice (giving up their birthday presents), and a vision that seems attainable but will probably always be "out there" somewhere. (Chapter 4, Section "The Dos and Don'ts", and Chapter 5 cover these aspects also.)

On the flip side, I attended a campaign-ending celebration event for key volunteers and while it was a nice evening, the program featured celebrity presenters, not the volunteers who made it all happen, and the climax of the night was to ask everyone there to send a text about their new initiative being launched that night, only two weeks after the campaign ended. It was all about asking us to do something for the cause. Sure, we were all engaged, but the charity missed the opportunity to give everyone a breather and simply thank them for their efforts.

Charity: water kept their thanks simple, personal, real, and funny. They made it about the giver. Each video actually makes you want to consider another gift, or at least remain in a community that prides itself in the accomplishments made possible by its donors.

FOR THE VOLUNTEER FUNDRAISER: LOOKING UNDER THE HOOD OF A CHARITY'S FINANCIAL PRACTICES

So you've read how the money flows to your charity's bank account from a technical standpoint, and hopefully you've tasted what it might be like to wow your supporters by uniquely thanking them for their gifts. But how about once it reaches the organization's budget? How well does the organization use the money, and how can you get at least a topline look? These are important questions that you, as a micro-fundraiser, may have or that your friends and family may ask about as you request their support. Likewise, if you're a professional fundraiser, you should check that your charity is listed, and listed properly, in the major charity guides. Following is a brief look at the big ones, and Appendix B includes a full chart of what's online and the functionalities of each.

In terms of the usual suspects—GuideStar, Charity Navigator, Better Business Bureau (BBB)—which is most reliable, and why should your nonprofit register on them?

Given its breadth of current and historic information, **Charity Navigator** is considered by some as the most reliable nonprofit online evaluation website. It offers its users access to open comments, nonprofits' financials, and an overview of the organization's leadership and mission. You can also track the organization's financial progression over time and see key financial metrics compared to other organizations that are of a similar size and mission.

After Charity Navigator you might want to check out **GuideStar,** arguably the second most reliable online evaluation site. GuideStar, however, charges fees for some services that you might find on Charity Navigator for free. One advantage to using GuideStar that you are not going to get with Charity Navigator is access to thousands of organizations' Form 990. In my opinion, this is a very big advantage if you know what to look for. You can learn about:

- Numbers of board members, employees, and volunteers

- Names of board members

- Compensation of officers and highest-paid employees

- Fundraising expenses incurred by the organization (if more than $15,000, in which case it lists the names and amounts of fundraising subcontractors, on Schedule G, Part I)

- How much was grossed and netted from special events (Schedule G, Part II)

- Part IX shows a "Statement of Functional Expenses" and is important for donors who want transparency in the organizations they support

- In the case of foundations, on Part XV, grants made— amounts and grantees' names; important not only for similar grant-seeking organizations but also for the enterprising micro-fundraiser who wants to seek a matching grant from a foundation to match her online efforts for a cause

- On foundations' 990s, Part IV shows Capital Gains and Losses for tax on investment income

- Foundations' 990s include a balance sheet at the end listing their assets, including stock positions. Again, those seeking transparency will want to have this functionality on a charity review site

In addition, GuideStar also provides reports that can analyze and compare one or multiple nonprofits. They also offer charity verification and compensation research services.

WHY YOU SHOULD CONSULT THESE SITES

According to the National Center for Charitable Statistics, there are over 1.5 million nonprofit organizations in the United States alone (Foundation Center, 2011).[24] Given the breadth of the nonprofit world as well as the distinctiveness of nonprofit organizations, it benefits both the donor and the cause being served to have access to these third-party, comprehensive, and objective reviews. Today, more than ever, donors can thoroughly assess a nonprofit's effectiveness and efficiency, leadership, and reputation by accessing the wealth of information that is provided on these sites. This level of industry transparency affords donors comfort and confidence that their dollars are going to benefit the cause they are passionate about. Over the past four or five years these evaluation sites have become more and more of an essential part to the giving process. Sean Stannard-Stockton, chief executive of Tactical Philanthropy Advisors, says that, "There is a mindset shift going on in philanthropy.

---

[24]Foundation Center. (2011, 12 20). *Foundation Center*. Retrieved 12 20, 2011, from Frequently Asked Questions: http://foundationcenter.org/getstarted/faqs/html/howmany.html

People want to know that their money is actually making a difference."[25] As with the user reviews that consumers find on Amazon, Yelp.com, or Hotels.com, donors and volunteers can make a more educated decision about how they are going to spend their time and money by gaining wisdom from other donors' experiences and feedback.

How To Use Online Evaluation Sites

Just like when you review any option, it's recommended that you use multiple sources to research the organization you are hoping to partner with. I'd recommend that you start with CharityNavigator.com and once you've assessed the financial health and reputation of an organization, see what people are saying on GuideStar. Download the latest Form 990 and at least see whether they're spending a lot on fundraising, among other key facts. The information presented on these two sites is fair, accurate, and objective. (They do not, however, have the current Form 990 for free.) Lastly, for most industry leaders and participants, these two sources act as the gold standard for nonprofit evaluation sites.

Charting Impact

Further, the BBB Wise Giving Alliance, GuideStar, and the Independent Sector launched a site for charities to track their progress and outcomes, so that by year-end they'll have news to share with supporters and potential donors. It's called Charting Impact.[26]

---

[25]Feldman, A. (2010, 1 21). *businessweek.com*. Retrieved 12 20, 2011, from Philanthrophy: http://www.businessweek. com/magazine/content/10_05/ b4165072434039.htm

[26]http://www.chartingimpact.org/

The site's purpose is: "...[to encourage] strategic thinking about how you will achieve your goals." It also creates a report that lets you share concise, detailed information about plans and progress with key stakeholders, including the public. It was designed with several benefits in mind, including:

- Encouraging people to invest their money, time, and attention in effective organizations.

- Helping your organization highlight the difference you make.

- Positioning your organization to work with and learn from other organizations.

- Helping your organization sharpen your approaches to making a difference.

The way it works is to ask charities to answer five questions against which they're judged for results. The questions are:

1. What is your organization aiming to accomplish?

2. What are your strategies for making this happen?

3. What are your organization's capabilities for doing this?

4. How will your organization know if you are making progress?

5. What have and haven't you accomplished so far?

The questions are not unlike those one might find when approaching a large independent foundation, or when report-ing to one. (Similar to these questions are the "Expanded

Drucker Questions" that Intelligent Philanthropy asks its profiled organizations to answer, and which they then post on reports. This website is summarized with the others in Appendix B.) When I worked for a graduate school of theology, we and many of our peer schools wrote grant applications and reports to The Lilly Endowment, a foundation that champions seminary education. Being one of the few that made large grants to a host of schools from many different ecclesial traditions, Lilly was perennially lobbied for funds, and heavily so. Whether to weed out grant-seekers who were not serious or to command a certain level of quality in proposals, or both, Lilly's grant applications often required us to write proposals of upwards of fifty pages. Similarly, the annual reports we wrote after receiving a grant could easily be twenty pages. When one got a grant, it was worth it. When one was declined, it was heartbreak.

Yet, with Charting Impact, though the process is much simpler, nonprofits going through the exercise will benefit from answering similarly probing questions that many of your major donors and board members will ask you in person anyway.

Charting Impact's own answers—for comparison—can be found on their website, the link to which is footnoted below.[27]

Additional Thoughts

While all these sites are a great resource for donors, they can also help the nonprofit that is being evaluated improve their bottom line and improve their everyday operations. Accountability and transparency can be powerful when donors,

---

[27]http://www.chartingimpact.org/about/our-report/

board members, and volunteers are granted access to how the resources of an organization are being put to use. While inviting critiques is often a daunting prospect, I would encourage organizations to ask their constituents to comment on their experience with the organization and the things they felt were done well as well as areas that need improvement.

Here's an idea for nonprofits: A client of mine asked a group of their donors to go to GuideStar and write a Personal Review (under the charity page Summary tab). The organization now has 108 comments for potential donors to read. Granted, it's a biased perspective (most are glowing in their tone), but many nonprofits aren't familiar enough with these sites' functionalities to know that options like this are available to create additional awareness and momentum, let alone donation revenue. The exercise was also a great opportunity for the nonprofit to ask its most faithful donors to help them in a non-financial way. It engaged them.

Another idea: Most people have their COO, CFO, accountant, or auditing firm fill out the 990 and even the text responses the form calls for. Part I, line 1 requires a brief summary of the organization's mission or most significant activities. Most nonprofits fill these out perfunctorily to fulfill IRS requirements. But this line, which is the first thing readers see, is a great opportunity to highlight your organization. Three Metropolitan State University professors wrote a paper, the link for which can be found on GuideStar, that outlines the opportunities and risks of this newer Form 990 (covering Tax Year 2008 and onward).

3

"Click to Confirm": The Best Ways to Give Online

"DON'T GO IT ALONE." THE ADVANTAGES OF RAISING MONEY ONLINE WITH OTHER PEOPLE

Filmmaker Jennifer Fox broke all kinds of records when she raised money through Kickstarter to finish her latest project. It's not surprising that on a list of dozens of tips on how to do online crowdfunding, her second reason (after going to family and friends for money, which is a Kickstarter must) was to "Build a team."[28]

My first experience raising money was also doing it as a team. Granted, we thought of ourselves simply as a bunch of kids.

It was Halloween in New York City. I was sxi, and we had our juice-box sized cardboard UNICEF containers along with our candy bags, and we traversed street and avenue to trick-or-treat and also ask fellow citizens for pennies or nickels (which actually counted for something in the late 1960s). There was a very satisfying *kerplunk* when they or we dropped the coins in the orange box.

I felt a little weird about this at first, but my younger brother and my friends who traveled with us (and a parent or two) did this together, so I quickly moved past my embarrassment. The only drawback was that it lessened our physical ability to hold our loot of candy.

When you are part of a fundraising team, there are at least four elements that are present that are lacking when you're on your own:

• Encouragement

• Accountability

• Friendly competition

• Fun

---

[28]Hope for Film blog. May 24, 2011. http://blogs.indiewire.com/tedhope/ guest_post_jennifer_fox_the_first_6_tips_for_launching_a_six-figure_kicksta

Convio, a leader in online fundraising and the group that helped New Hampshire Governor Howard Dean raise more money online in the run-up to the 2004 presidential election than had ever been raised, has metrics to show the effectiveness of going it alone versus raising money in a team.

They use the example of "Event Fundraising" like walk-a-thons, and separate them into non-competitive, competitive, and endurance races.

Here are the differences in what people raise when alone versus in a team:

Source: Convio[29]	Non-competitive "a-thon"	Competitive "a-thon"	Endurance race
Solo	$52	$28	$611
Team	$79	$49	$1091

The data say it all: when you're raising money alongside friends or peers, it's better for the organization sponsor. It's also probably more fun for you, the fundraiser, to gain more support.

It's worth noting that the non-competitive walks or fun runs, many of them with no registration fee, raise more money on average than the timed 5K or 10K races that are typical of the competitive category.

If you're in charge of designing a program, you'll have to decide whether the combined fees plus a lower average fundraising total (regardless of solo solicitors or team efforts) will be more fruitful for you than a free event where you

---

[29]http//www.convio.com/our-research/infographics/event-fundraising.html

encourage (but don't require) people to raise money. Also consider the primary purpose: is it to raise money, build your mailing list, both, or some other purpose?

But be ready, fundraisers: Convio claims that it takes five emails to secure one donation. (That is, for every five recipients who receive your appeal, one will say "yes.") The average total number of emails ranges from twenty-five (competitive) to thirty-one (non-competitive) to ninety-eight (endurance).

When I participated in the "Live Below the Line" Campaign (see Introduction), I sent about 1,200 emails and had 85 donors, which is below average, but I threw the net as wide as possible by going to my entire mailing list.

There also has long been the practice of "giving circles," which are more common among women than men, and more common in non-Western cultures.

ONE WORD: PLASTIC

We want to turn now to the efficiency and costs of raising money online. Part of that is the cost of using credit cards and online gift processing. But first, a look at online fundraising alongside its sibling strategies, and a caveat.

Waste can occur in both the methods charities use to raise money as well as in their stewardship of gifts once received. The website Supporting Advancement has numerous helpful resources, not least of which are good benchmarks around "the cost of a dollar raised."

The site points to James Greenfield's 1999 book, *Fund-Raising: Evaluating and Managing the Fund Development Process*, which was written before the boom in online giving. Supporting Advancement notes that the overall national average cost to raise a dollar (CTRD) is **20 cents**; that is, 80 cents of every dollar raised goes to the charitable purpose/programs. Here's how they list different methods within the fundraising operation (these would be at a well-established organization):

1. **Capital Campaign/Major Gifts:** $0.05 to $0.10 per dollar raised.

2. **Corporations and Foundations (Grant Writing):** $0.20 per dollar raised.

3. **Direct Mail Renewal:** $0.20 per dollar raised.

4. **Planned Giving:** $0.25 per dollar raised.

5. **Benefit/Special Events:** $0.50 of gross proceeds.

6. **Direct Mail Acquisition:** $1.00 to $1.25 per dollar raised (yes, can be net negative).

7. **National Average:** $0.20.

I would slightly tweak two benchmarks above and add one more, though none of this is an exact science.[30] First, given

---

[30]For further information, see The Jossey-Bass Handbook of Nonprofit Leadership & Management 2nd Ed. (Robert D. Herman & Associates, editors; San Francisco: Jossey-Bass; 2005, p. 429). Here writer Robert Fogal correctly points out that "New Donor Acquisition" can cost up to $1.50 per dollar raised—yes, it's a money loser if you do it by direct mail—and planned giving costs up to $0.15 per dollar raised, assuming at least five years' initial investment. He agrees with the figures for Major Gifts, Special Events, and Foundation grantseeking.

the relative size of gifts coming from planned giving efforts, the cost of raising these gifts is more efficient than cited here and is probably closer to $0.15 to $0.20 on the dollar raised. Also, since bequests often go into endowment and provide interest, those gifts are effectively even cheaper over time.

Second, special events are indeed costly. Other sources might raise? the cost closer to $0.30 on the dollar raised, but any way you calculate it, this form of fundraising is in many ways the least efficient. One way to consider lowering your event costs is through online registration. Two notable tools are EventBrite, which touts helping sold more than 44 million tickets; and Ticket Cake, which launched at the Sundance Film Festival in Park City, Utah and sees itself as a partner with charities rather than merely a ticket-selling vendor. Charities using these and other vendors can often gain access to ticket-buyer information (name/address), since most of us use credit cards to buy tickets. Using an online ticketing tool, therefore, helps maximize future donations and also reduces the soft cost of staff or volunteers doing registration by hand. As we all know, you can use these kinds of tools to remind people of the event coming up and reduce attrition, something nearly impossible to do at scale with staff for a large event without incurring huge costs. Large nonprofit software companies like Blackbaud and Convio can include special events functionalities that have sophisticated event registration and reminder systems.

For all the negatives surrounding cost, special events are still very effective for engaging new donors with your organization and—in the case of annual gala dinners—introducing potential new board members to the organization as well as building and maintaining good public relations.

The one fundraising method missing above (aside from our topic at hand) is telemarketing or holding a telethon. If hired for fundraising, telemarketers can take as much as 75% of what is raised. Most donors don't realize this and very few want to get the call in the first place. When schools and membership organizations choose to call their supporters annually for gifts, however, there is often more than money gained. The alumna being called can talk to a student, for instance, and relive her days on campus before making her annual pledge. There are soft costs to training the student caller, but again, missional objectives are achieved beyond mere dollars raised.

In my opinion, the best use of the phone is to call supporters when you want to thank them, and *only* thank them. You should leave a message if you get an answering machine. Whether you're a senior officer or nonprofit executive director calling a lead donor to say thank-you, or a student calling an alum after a $100 annual fund gift is received, to have someone call simply to express gratitude without asking for anything further is refreshingly counter-cultural (like the charity: water thank-you videos mentioned earlier). Don't be surprised if conducting a "thank-a-thon" some February after year-end gifts have come in doesn't leave your supporters even more connected to you than ever.

With online gift processing, the normal benchmark is set between $0.03 and $0.08 on the dollar raised. I say "gift processing," because the true cost of raising a dollar online will include your website, which has many non-fundraising costs associated with it, as well as your database and email costs, which also are not exclusively used for fundraising. These gift-processing costs are covered below.

Now there's a caveat to this kind of analysis from MalWarwick,[31] the legendary nonprofit consultant and author. He writes that the "overall fundraising 'cost to raise a dollar' is a myth. There is NO such standard, and anyone who tells you there is one should survey the real world of fundraising in all its diversity. One organization might be embarrassed to spend more than a dime to raise a dollar, while another might be fortunate to squeak by with $0.40 or $0.50 cents on a dollar—and both might be ethically-run, well-managed organizations."

This is a separate subject entirely, and readers can also go to Intelligent Philanthropy, which is a new website that allows donors to look at fundraising effectiveness and not just fundraising efficiency.

The issue here is efficiency. Undeniably, raising money online is more efficient. And, online giving is of course more and more prevalent, even for larger gifts.

"With our generation, it's going to be more online giving in the future," says a 34-year-old mom of two, married to a busy 40-year-old energy trader in Houston.[32] This statement alone shouldn't be a surprise. But when you learn that this couple makes yearly six-figure gifts to a number of charities—online— our ears as professionals and fellow givers should perk up.

Granted, these larger gifts online are rare. And this couple makes gifts after doing due diligence, both through the organization's website and also through online watchdog groups like Charity Navigator (see Chapter 2, Section "For the Volunteer Fundraiser: Looking Under the Hood of a Charity's

---

[31]See Warwick's website: malwarwick.com.
[32]Source: Chronicle of Philanthropy. May 1, 2011

Financial Practices" for a summary of these groups). They don't give randomly. Yet, what can organizations do to prepare for these kinds of large gifts?

Sometimes it's a matter of making sure your site can handle the extra zeroes.

"We have given to charities over the past five years, and only about half can take that large a donation online," the donor said.[33]

And what would cause a donor to hesitate before making a large gift, or any at all for that matter?

"If a website or contact information isn't updated, it makes you wonder what other aspects of the organization are neglected."

This couple obviously feels secure making significant online financial transactions. But as a giver, you might not. And as a nonprofit leader, you might not want to incur the costs that are summarized below.

Most costs associated with traditional (offline) fundraising are fairly straightforward. If you're sending a direct mail piece, you know what the postage is going to be and what the cost of supplies is going to be. If you're planning an event, you know you've got to cover food, drink, and SWAG ("Stuff We All Get") bag items. But if you're raising support through your website or a third-party merchant service provider (see

---

[33]Gifts at $100,000 are obviously quite rare. Blackbaud, in its 2010 Online Giving Report, cites that among the 1,812 charities whose online giving results it tracks, $100,000 is the largest gift experienced by any of them. That said, 88% of study participants experienced at least one online gift of $1,000 or more, which is up from 77% in 2009. You can get the whole report here: https://www.blackbaud.com/bb/online/fundraising

below), it can be difficult to assess your costs—especially the recurring ones—unless you read the fine print. Today there are a number of online giving platforms and merchant service providers that have made fundraising easy and efficient for both the donor and the fundraiser. These providers give fundraisers a platform to better reach your donors, infuse excitement into the fundraising process, provide donors with a variety of ways to make gifts, and report back to your supporters how their gifts were used. What fundraisers often don't see are the costs that go into these services. The first step in assessing which provider to use is to ask yourself four questions about your charity:

1. What kind of institution or cause do you represent? Are you a one-person outfit trying to raise a small amount of support, or are you backed by a historical institution that is trying to fund a $10 million annual budget? From there you can better assess what you are willing to pay for. Smaller institutions might want to find a platform that can scale with it, which most can (e.g., "Basic," "Professional," and "Premium" levels, and so on, at increasing costs).

2. What do you need to have a successful campaign? Ask yourself what kind of fundraising elements you or your volunteer fundraisers want and need:

   • Integration with social media?

   • Website design?

   • Data analytics and reporting?

   • Integration with your enterprise database?

- Ability to accept recurring gifts or bank drafts (ACH/EFT)?

- Donor marketing support?

3. What is the difference between an "online giving platform" and a "merchant service provider"? And who are the ideal charities to use each?

Online Giving Platform – Typically online giving platforms offer an all-in-one service to a fundraiser. They can handle everything from e-marketing strategies to processing your gifts. This type of provider is normally best suited for a cause-focused fundraiser who doesn't have the luxury of being backed by an established institution (Not so good for large institutions or scaled membership-driven associations). They are also appropriate for one-off efforts by smaller or mid-sized organizations that don't want to invest in creating a solution and then owning it. Think of it as the Zip Car of online giving solutions. A list of these is in Appendix A.

Merchant Service Provider – These providers typically do not offer the additional value-added services that an online giving platform might offer. They normally only deal with the processing of your gift and in turn tend to be a cheaper option. The ideal user would be an organization that already has a website and a range of distribution channels. Large organizations have the budget to hire a solution-provider and have a fully branded online giving platform that is integrated with their site and their enterprise database or CRM system. They still need, however, a functionality to help them process gifts, which this tool serves as.

4. What are the basic fees charged by online-giving platform and merchant service providers?

Setup Fees – These fees might include branding your organization's website or creating custom donation forms. Or it might include neither and be strictly a fee to begin using their service.

Monthly/Annual Fees – These normally cover the cost of donor communication pieces, whether through email or direct mail. They also normally cover automatic receipting and customer service support.

Processing Fees – This fee is often the most substantial and can range from 2.19 to 7.5%, depending on what additional services your provider offers. It is important to budget this expense into your planning. If your project goal is $10,000 online and your provider is charging you 5%, you actually need to raise $10,500 to cover processing fees. If you are a smaller budget organization, and a lot of your gifts come online, this applies to you in particular. I know of a start-up whose budget is $200,000 and they get 65% of their donation revenue from online gifts. A variance in any of these fees, scaled this way and impacting this small budget, can make a real difference in their program funding. It also can make a difference when they send the annual report to donors and list the cost of fundraising.

Transaction Fees – Again, depending on who your provider is, this may or may not be an issue. The transaction fee is a fixed fee that is assessed on each gift you receive and normally ranges from $0.10 to $0.30. Taking our example above of a project goal of $10,000.

Assume we had 500 donors make gifts of $20 each. The transaction fee was $0.30 each and there was a processing fee of 5% for each transaction as well. This would result in an extra $150 in transaction fees and $500 in processing fees, leaving you with $9,350 from $10,000 in gifts. Your new total needed would be $10,650 to cover the cost of your project.

Three examples of providers whose fees are not readily identifiable are Causes.com (4.75%), Ammado (5%–7.5%), and GlobalGiving (15%). If users look closely enough they can find these fees on these providers' FAQ pages. Also, be aware of current U.S. legislation (the Durbin amendment of the Dodd-Frank Act in particular), which affects how debit cards can be used in financial transactions, including charitable giving. According to an August 2011 article in Financial Reform Insights,[34] the permissible fees for debit card transactions are as follows:

- A base fee of $0.21 per transaction for transactional type costs/expenditures

- A five-basis-point adjustment to cover potential losses from fraudulent activity

- An additional $0.01 per transaction fee to cover fraud prevention costs (except for monitoring, which is included in the base transaction costs/expenditures noted above) if the issuer is eligible

---

[34]http://www.financialreforminsights.com/2011/08/02/final-durbin-amendment-%e2%80%9ccaps%e2%80%9d-debit-card-interchange-fees/#.TvH8r9HzVc8.email

The article states that "[in] 2009, the average debit card transaction was approximately $40. Based on the final permissible fee structure, the interchange fee applicable to this transaction would be capped at $0.24 ($0.21 + ($40 X .05) + $0.01)." Of course, this applies to banks that have more than $10 billion in assets. The same cap does not apply to smaller banks issuing debit cards. (I can see your eyes glazing over.)

Additional Notes: Just now and throughout this book, you've heard the term "interchange fee" (which is what credit card companies charge on each credit/debit card transaction). Each transaction with a Visa or MasterCard typically involves five parties: the purchaser, the seller, the Visa or MasterCard, the bank that sponsors the card, and the card processor. Among credit cards, only Visa and MasterCard carry interchange fees. American Express and Discover do not participate in interchange, because they themselves are the issuing bank, the merchant bank, and the card association, so they handle all aspects of the card transaction and don't require the same fees.[35]

Merchants (like your local grocery store) do not pay interchange fees; they pay a "merchant discount" to their financial institution. This is an important distinction, because merchants buy a variety of processing services from financial institutions; all these services may be included in their merchant discount rate, typically a percentage rate per transaction. Fundraisers who are set up to receive gifts online must first pay a credit card processor, who then pays the credit card

---

[35]Some online giving platforms listed in Appendix A offer lower fees if a donor uses American Express or Discover, but some platforms require a fixed fee regardless. Please check with the vendor and get all fees in writing.

company an additional fee. Processors normally charge organizations a percentage of each bill, which means 1.61%–6.5%, plus an additional flat rate per credit card gift ($0.20-$0.23). A base rate of 2% is pretty good. Ask your online giving platform provider if they can use your existing merchant card processor (if you already have one). Be wary of extremely low fees, such as less than 1.5%. A card processor might be also tacking on a monthly fee and a transaction fee, and you should read their FAQs and also ask them. Get all fees in writing.

If you are a nonprofit, consider asking your donors to add to their donation the equivalent of the processing fee. Some platforms themselves offer this option (GlobalGiving and Network for Good[36]), which is extremely helpful to the nonprofit, and givers won't usually mind giving a few extra dollars when they know it helps defray administrative costs.

TELL A FRIEND: LEVERAGING THE POWER OF CROWDS

According to Jeff Howe, an innovator in the field, crowdsourcing is "when a company takes a job that was once performed by employees and outsources it in the form of an open-call to a large undefined group of people generally using the Internet."[37] Howe succinctly sums up the idea of crowdsourcing, for that cocktail conversation, as "Wikipedia, with everything."

Howe uses the example of photography. He says that with the advent of cheaper digital SLR cameras, software to manipulate

---

[36]See Wall Street Journal, Dec 17, 2011, page B8. http://online.wsj.com/article/SB10001424052970203518404577096793924531200.html?KEYWORDS=online+giving
[37]Good video on the subject at http://crowdsourcing

images, and the Internet, the number of stock photos increased exponentially, and what was once the proving ground of the experts is now the playground of all. The commodity price of stock photos then of course plummeted. Given this trend in the private sector, Howe says that while crowdsourcing doesn't eradicate a business where crowdsourcing is now the norm (like stock photography), it changes that business: "companies [must now] approach us as potential partners."

Howe also notes the emergence of the online community as "the building block of crowdsourcing." People can "self-organize into productive units."

While our discussion here won't include how charities can ask the crowd about branding and products, nonprofits rely more and more on the power of crowds for everything from donations to volunteers and event attendance, which all operate online similarly as corporate crowdsourcing. We've discussed elsewhere how peer-to-peer asking and recruiting is more powerful and successful than organization-driven, top-down oriented communication. Crowdsourcing is all about engaging the community, and as it takes on a life of its own, community members "own" the process and derive some of the best ideas for—in this case—sustainable donation revenue. Additionally, there is a deep cultural history of donors and volunteers formally and informally partnering with a voluntary charitable association dating back at least to the mid-19th century when Toqueville toured America and found a plethora of people affiliating with one another to get things done or just to hang out together.

When the March of Dimes launched its walk-a-thon in 1970 as a community fundraiser, it was securing donation revenue by leveraging the crowd, and the crowd's smaller crowds (their friends who sponsored them).[38] People in the community became engaged with their feet, their hearts, and their pocketbooks. They engaged their friends and neighbors. It succeeded through a community effort, and the effort strengthened the community.

In fact, among Gen X and Gen Y donors, Convio found that nearly 90% indicated that a "friend asking a friend" for money to sponsor them in a race, etc., is an "appropriate channel of solicitation."[39] While this could be categorized more correctly as peer-to-peer fundraising (which is what our parents did in person over expensive meals), it nevertheless includes the distinctions of being an *open-call* to an *undefined group*.

TRULY "GLOBAL GIVING": TAPPING INTO WORLDWIDE RESOURCES

IRL (In Real Life): An online effort after a bus tour around the country

Based in Queensland, Tania Major is an Aboriginal Australian,

the 2007 Young Australian of the Year, and is demonstrating the power of micro-fundraising as a burgeoning community builder there.

Among her many personal and professional initiatives,

---

[38]http://www.marchofdimes.com/mission/history_indepth.html
[39]Convio. "Next Generation of American Giving" March 2010.

she is the top online fundraiser for the Australian Literacy and Numeracy Foundation. ALNF teaches marginalized Australians—including those in refugee and indigenous communities—how to read and write. A non-governmental organization called Generation One took Major as a spokesperson for the group along with other leaders on a three-month bus tour all over Australia. To build their mailing list of people to get involved in the cause, they asked for names, addresses, and email addresses, resulting in a list of more than 200,000 people. Generation One has begun working on a number of initiatives, helping Major with her efforts

in ALNF's "Wall of Hands" online fundraising initiative.

"There's a massive sea change of generous people who want to help," Major said. "More and more Australians are willing to contribute." Yet, she says that "philanthropy is still relatively new here."

At the end of 2011, ALNF was already up to nearly AUS $160,000 in online donations. The strong community created by Generation One's bus tour was one reason why ALNF has benefited from Major's online efforts.

We Americans are accustomed to considering ourselves to be the most philanthropic nation on earth.[40] Now, we *do* give away a lot of money, in absolute terms and even per capita, and fundraising in this country dates back to 1636 and the early support around Harvard College. But generosity is not defined solely by money, and generosity as defined by

---

[40]For more information on global trends, particularly in Australia where many trends are started, connect with Michael Buoy on LinkedIn and "Online Fundraising for Australian Nonprofits."

something like hospitality is a deep and ancient cultural value in areas such as the Middle East and in sub-Saharan Africa. Likewise, Latin America has *simpatia,* expressed toward the poor, which includes not only money but a certain sense of cultural responsibility. In fact, it is not the wealthiest nations that are most "generous" but rather those countries and peoples who are "happiest" and have the greatest sense of well-being and security.

The U.K.-based Charities Aid Foundation publishes the annual "World Giving Index"[41] with Gallup that tracks generosity with three metrics: giving money, volunteering time, and helping a stranger. In late 2011, the newest CAF report came out, placing the USA in the #1 spot; Ireland as #2, Australia #3 and New Zealand #4. Regionally speaking, though, Australasia (Australia and New Zealand) still tops North America (U.S., Canada) for overall composite giving score. In 2010, Australia and New Zealand were tied at #1, and the U.S. was #5.

Another encouraging statistic from the 2011 report is the trend in giving among age groups. The 25 to 34-year-old group (obviously heavy users of the Internet) had a global uptick of 0.5% in giving money. Those aged 15 to 24 and 35 to 49 declined slightly. People aged 50 and up also increased in their giving. Groups like Global Poverty Project are specifically and wisely targeting this younger demographic

---

[41] Found on the Charities Aid Foundation website: https://www.cafonline. org/research/publications/2010-publications/world Americans who want to get more resources on fundraising and giving elsewhere might try CAF's U.S. office in Virginia (info@cafamerica.org), or go to www.cafamerica. org.

as change agents, reaching them via the Internet through microfundraising campaigns like the "Live Below the Line"[42] effort discussed earlier. Such efforts also tap into a visceral sense of community, a quiet narrative that occurs in each of us as we enter our twenties and want to make our mark.

In 2010, the country that boasted the highest percentage (83%) of citizens who said they gave away money in the previous month was tiny Malta, in the Mediterranean, where some readers will recall St. Paul was shipwrecked for four months in the late 1st century A.D. This past year, it was Thailand, and the United States and Malta tied at tenth place. The Thai-Asean News Network attributed their #1 ranking to a strong and unified community: "Thailand's ranking resulted from the assistance given during the severe flooding, as Thais united to help each other in the flood predicament."[43] Similarly, many Americans will recall the flooding in Nashville, Tennessee, in May 2010. It was the most costly non-hurricane disaster to hit an American city. A blogger expressed the Nashville community ethos when writing:

> Today, I heard a soundbite of Anderson Cooper on CNN…expressing quite a bit of surprise at how much and how quickly people were going in to help their neighbors, fellow citizens and complete strangers. He was surprised by the generous spirit of the Nashville and Tennessee people. Surprised by what? That they care? Or that they bother to help, even if it isn't their own home?

---

[42]http://www.livebelowtheline.com/about/

[43]http://www.thailandoutlook.tv/tan/ViewData.aspx?DataID=1050896

Frankly, I am not the least bit surprised. It's what we try to do.

Moving on...[44]

When people are happy and have a sense of well-being, they help others.

I mention the World Giving Index data and the anecdotes mainly so that we can take a broader look at generosity and fundraising efforts in various locations across the globe, learning about what works elsewhere and why and perhaps applying it in the U.S.

First, donors everywhere want to make sure that the non-profits they're giving to are legitimate and that their gifts are being used wisely. We touched on this process in the U.S. in Chapter 2, Section "For the Volunteer Fundraiser: Looking Under the Hood of a Charity's Financial Practices." The Canada-based CharityVillage.com[45] publishes a list of watchdog organizations for donors and grantmakers in Canada, Europe, Japan, and Australian (as well as the U.S.). Likewise, in the U.K. there is Charity Commission.[46] Also universal among donors is the awareness of the connectedness between philanthropy and community. Here's what donor advisory group Philanthropy Australia says on its website:

"Philanthropy Australia is the national peak body for philanthropy and is a not-for-profit membership organisation. Our

---

[44]http://saintseestersays.saintseester.com/?p=1022
[45]http://www.charityvillage.com/cv/guides/guide8.asp
[46]http://www.charity-commission.gov.uk/

members are trusts and foundations, families and individuals who want to make a difference through their own philanthropy and to encourage others to become philanthropists.

"Our mission is to represent, grow and inspire an effective and robust philanthropic sector for the community."[47]

Certainly, this group's vision is not unique among groups that advocate for generosity. Such groups not only make grants but also want to teach philanthropy (don't just give away the fish; teach others to fish and give away the fish).

Yet, Australia and New Zealand in many ways both set the standard and also exemplify what philanthropy is at its best: an individual's response to a need as well as an encouragement for others to do likewise.

Three sites more commonly used than others in Australia, according to fundraisers there who lead LinkedIn discussion groups, are Artez, Go Fundraise, and Everyday Hero (which has been purchased by Blackbaud). Each is detailed in Appendix A.

Based in Queensland, online fundraising platform Everyday Hero appeals to the aspect of philanthropy that groups like charity: water have found to be effective—make donors a central part of the charity's story and success. As they put it, "you will always be heroes to the people you have helped. […] We see that basically all human beings care about their community, environment and fellow man, and will contribute towards creating a better world to bring their children into if they

---

[47]http://www.philanthropy.org.au

have the means." Effective charities try to make it as simple as possible for donors to give and micro-fundraisers to raise money from their friends and family. Everyday Hero claims that 30% of the people who are emailed will donate to the micro-fundraiser's cause.

As Adelaide-based eCommerce consultant Michael Bouy[48] notes, and this is true of nonprofits everywhere, while some of Australia's largest charities use the above platforms, many will develop their own so that they don't have to pay a third party.

Another option for givers, and in this case Canadian givers, is a very simple online donor-advised fund (like a mini-foundation, stewarded by large financial institutions and from which donors can make designated gifts; often abbreviated DAF) called "Chimp," based in Vancouver. This book will not cover DAFs, but a visit to Chimp is quite a different feel than a visit to Fidelity, Vanguard, or Oppenheimer, and it simply "feels" more like an online giving platform. It's a DAF, no doubt, but given our lives' movement onto the Internet, even DAFs are affording the feel of personal control found in a micro-fundraising site and are influenced by Apple-inspired design sensibilities.

We read about worthy causes in other countries but find that we can't make charitable donations to them because of legal issues. Likewise, American ex-pats have their own issues (tax-related and otherwise) donating money while overseas. Around

---

[48]Bouy runs a site called CharitiesHouse.com and formerly served as eCommerce manager for The Salvation Army Australia Southern Territory.

the globe, possible donors looking for philanthropic solutions are limited by what you might call the lack of "portability" of philanthropy across national borders.

The Berkley, California-based Half the Sky Foundation (caring for China's orphans) is one group that has established operating units in various countries, notably in Hong Kong (where there are two types of charity operations, one being a fairly low maintenance entity not requiring an operating Board of Directors). They now can receive contributions from six countries. If your U.S. nonprofit serves a non-U.S. population, even in part, there are ways to receive local donations from philanthropists. This is especially important in emerging markets and also in countries where the culture is to donate locally.

4

The "Toolbox"

When you open a toolbox, you find a lot objects that look different in shape and size but are there because you need to fix something, improve it, or build it.

The following chapters are each here to help explain the online tools as well as some general fundraising principles that will make your fundraising experience more rewarding. Some are online-oriented, and some are knowledge-based tools that you need for your online work.

It is hoped that they will either help you fix, improve, or build.

THE TOP 10 FUNDRAISING PLATFORMS (FULL LIST IS APPENDIX A)

"Top 10"

- **Razoo.** *Pros:* There are no set-up, monthly, or transaction fees associated with this provider. In addition to being a low cost option, it also offers two very distinct giving tools: the ability to give through Facebook and the Razoo mobile giving app. *Cons:* Razoo does not allow for recurring gifts or gifts via EFTs.

- **Causes.** *Pros:* Easy to set up, and it provides fundraisers with the ability to access their network of supporters directly through Facebook and Twitter. Gifts are processed through Network For Good,[49] which allows your donors to make gifts using American Express, MasterCard, and Visa. It also allows you to set up recurring gifts. There are no set-up or monthly fees. *Cons:* The processing fee is 4.75%, which is on the higher end, but you have to remember that you're not paying a set-up, monthly, or transaction fee.

- **Network for Good.** *Pros:* Integrated with Facebook, Twitter, LinkedIn, StumbleUpon, and Google. They also provide the donor with the option of covering the processing and transaction fees. *Cons:* depending on what your needs are, the set-up cost can be up to $200 with a monthly fee of $50. So unless you need some of their value-added services, it might get expensive.

---

[49]Katya Andreson, author of Robin Hood Marketing, referred to throughout this book, is VP for Marketing here.

- **Ammado.** *Pros:* This provider is integrated into all major social media networks, accepts all major credit cards, and can handle gifts in 75 different currencies. *Cons:* The total processing fee can range from 5% to 7.5%.

- **JustGive.** *Pros:* This is an inexpensive option that accepts all major credit cards and they help individuals find charities to support. Supporters can also write reviews about your organization. *Cons:* They do not accept e-checks (ACH/EFT) or gifts of stock.

- **Givezooks!** *Pros:* This provider is very customizable and can process all major credit cards and EFTs. *Cons:* The only reason this provider is not rated higher is because of the monthly fee of $125. This is a premium provider, but most people will find that fee hard to stomach.

- **SeeYourImpact.** *Pros:* They accept all major credit cards, eChecks, and you can set up recurring gifts. Also, your donors get to see a picture and profile of the person or group they helped. *Cons:* This platform acts only as a giving platform, no other value-added service.

- **Crowdrise.** *Pros:* This provider is similar to Facebook in that you create your own profile but with philanthropic info. Points are awarded that can be redeemed for prizes such as clothing, electronics, etc. *Cons:* The processing and transaction fees can be on the high side, 4% to 5% and $1 to $2.50 respectively.

- **YourCause.com.** *Pros:* 3% transaction fee, regardless of card, and it is integrated with Facebook, LinkedIn, and

Twitter. *Cons:* Acts only as a giving platform, so no value-added service.

- **DonorsChoose.com.** *Pros:* This provider accepts all major credit cards and eChecks. *Cons:* They only support teacher-sponsored educational projects.

"Briefly Noted"

Also worth mentioning separately are a couple big dogs in the pack and a newcomer to the scene:

- **Convio.** This is the tool that in many ways revolutionized online community building and giving, especially among the under-35-year-old set. Running for president, Vermont governor Howard Dean raised more than $14 million in the third quarter of 2003, much of it in online gifts of less than $80. Convio helped make this happen. In 2008, the company consulted on President Obama's record-breaking online fundraising efforts. Fully integratable with all social media. The Mercedes of online giving and community building solutions and priced as such. Also check out its new tool Common Ground Social, which is important if you want to track, capture, and store/integrate certain activity into your customer relationship management (CRM) system.

- **eTapestry.** This platform is owned by Blackbaud,[50] a company that serves perhaps more nonprofits in its various software solutions than any other. Blackbaud white papers

---

[50]Blackbaud, owner of eTapestry, is in the process of acquiring Convio, as this book goes to press. Readers should check with companies on their policies and pricing structures.

are some of the best around (as are Convio's), so being a customer connects you with the leading thought in online giving. Their "Starter" kit is $99.

- **CauseVox.** This is a newer platform with low up-front costs and transaction fees and which allows for branded campaigns. It has a clean look-and-feel and good customer service. They also regularly produce helpful accompanying blog and e-newsletters and white papers. CauseVox is a good solution for smaller nonprofits or start-ups.

Our Australian colleagues report that nonprofits there—including the larger ones—occasionally use platforms such as **Artez, GoFundraise** and **Everyday Hero** (covered in Appendix A and touched on in Chapter 3, Section "Truly "Global Giving": Tapping into Worldwide Resources"), but for most efforts and since they can afford it, they will pay a provider to developed a solution they own instead of paying a recurring fee.[51]

ONLINE PAYMENT SOLUTIONS

Still other nonprofits, rather than conduct a campaign, may be looking simply for an online payment solution. Most of the following are tools for e-commerce but can often serve to receive charitable gifts. Nonprofits should compare their needs alongside the tool's functionalities. More tools come online all the time, and a Google search will always give you the most up to date information.

---

[51]Indebted to the folks at Online Fundraising for Australian Nonprofits, created by Michael Bouy.

Some popular payment tools[52] that have stood the test of time so far include:

- **PayPal.** This has become almost ubiquitous in use and the industry standard, alongside Amazon Payments. Audiences are familiar with it and trust it. It has good brand presence and lends its brand credibility to a site that uses it, and is therefore good for smaller organizations that want a proven tool without a lot of start-up hassle. Yet its monthly and transaction fees can get expensive.

- **Click & Pledge.** (Also has giving platform functionalities.) Delivering fairly sophisticated online and mobile giving tools, Click & Pledge also offers additional functionalities for community building as well as donor contact management. They charge a 4.75% fee on each transaction, which is significant if receiving larger transactions. This can add 25% or more to the cost of raising a dollar for many organizations. It's best for the mid-size to large institution that has a team who can structure and implement it.

- **GiftTool.** Offers donation, membership, event registration, and a-thon tools. They are based in Canada and used more in that country than in U.S.

- **MemberClicks.** More of a membership management system—albeit an intuitive one geared toward "small staffs"— that partners with online payment tools, such as Moolah.

- **Moolah.** Made by OurSiteSolutions, this product is used mainly to monetize websites and sell products.

---

[52]Source: FundraisingSuccess.com; October 2007.

- **CharityWeb.** Larger organizations with a budget for customized solutions have used this tool, yet so have smaller groups. For example, it's used by Make-a-Wish Foundation and Caring Bridge, which work at scale, but not many others who do likewise. Regional groups and some houses of worship use it to integrate membership and giving.

- **GreaterGiving.** (Used to be called AuctionPay.) Good for schools and nonprofits that engage in large numbers of online gifts, online auctions, event check-in/registration, or a-thons where people are signing up or sponsoring others.

- **GoogleCheckout.** (Has some giving platform functionality.) A Chicago-based nonprofit has been using this tool almost exclusively for the past two years and has saved more than $6,000 in fees. They claim it's very easy to use. The fees start at 2.9% + $0.30 for total monthly transactions less than $3,000 and decrease as monthly total transactions increase. (See more details on platform summary in Appendix A.)

- **Acceptiva.** Unlike other tools that also act as website monetizers, Acceptiva specializes in nonprofits. It's good for donations, gifts to houses of worship, tuition payments to schools, event registrations (including a-thons), tribute gifts ("in memory of"), and ticket sales.

THE 10 MOST GOOGLED CHARITIES OR GIVING OPPORTUNITIES (AND WHY THAT'S IMPORTANT...)

When you type in "donate" to Google, you'll get 430,000,000 results in 0.38 seconds. So, what's a humble charity to do to get some attention?

Each year, Google releases its "Zeitgeist Report" that shows searches in different categories. A fascinating look at this is found at Googlezeitgeist.com.[53] Here's a list of the top ten phrases in the "charitable giving" category in U.S. Google searches (input to Google's search window):

1. Donate to Japan

2. Red Cross Japan

3. Japan Relief

4. South Sudan

5. Second Mile Foundation

6. Goodwill Donation Center

7. Joe Corbi

8. Headstart

9. Make A Wish

10. Salvation Army Donations

What conclusions can we make?

Internet searches result from a need for immediate information (e.g. Japan relief topping the list), and online giving flows from that.

---

[53]The interactive graphic for charity searches can be found at http://www.googlezeitgeist.com/en/top-lists/us/humanities/fastest-rising-charitable-giving

The corollary to this is that you could be missing a lot of donation revenue if your charity is chartered to respond to crises programmatically but has a website that lacks aesthetics or the proper donation functionalities.

Likewise, proper search engine optimization (SEO; see Introduction) will allow your organization to take advantage of searches for phrases and words that direct users to your site to make donations.

Certain organizations have such strong brands—Red Cross, Goodwill, Head Start, Make-a-Wish, Salvation Army—that when people think to make a difference, they simply put the words that come most quickly. Your brand needs to be synonymous with the need your organization fills, so that online searches can lead people to your site to make a gift.

Certainly some searches, as for Red Cross, lead to further online activity like donating money. Other searches, such as for Goodwill, might lead to offline activity like driving to a clothing drop-off location. You can look to see how certain words commonly used by your organization are searched online at Google.[54] For instance, the word "donation" means different things to different people. First, it's much more searched in the United States than elsewhere. It also quite often refers to blood, plasma, organs, eggs, and cars, rather than money. "Charitable giving" is used most in the United States, with Canada and the U.K. a distant second and third. (Professionals and givers in the U.K., by the way, see "charity" and "scheme" yoked together as normative and neutral, and few if any English-speaking countries search using this

---

[54]http://www.google.com/insights/search/

phrase.) Further, "charitable giving" is mostly a Northeastern U.S. and Midwestern phrase. Massachusetts, and Boston specifically, takes the lead in using this search term.

"Fundraising," however, is searched more commonly in Kenya and Australia than in the U.S., with New Zealand in fourth. In Kenya, the word suddenly shot into the stratosphere around September 2007. This likely had to do with President Obama's Kenyan heritage. Also in Kenya, the term common among Christians—"tithing"—is searched most there out of any country, followed by South Africa, then the United States, the Philippines, and New Zealand. In the U.S., residents in Utah far and away search this term more than anyone, followed by those in Idaho, seven Southeastern and Deep South states, and one Great Plains state. (A sidenote to readers belonging to the Mormon Church: you've probably already learned that you can't easily give online to the LDS. One website, Mormon Life Hacker, has a way to set up your billpay to be able to give, so that you don't have to remember to bring your checkbook.)

Googling "giving" yields predictable results: each November the term spikes sharply and then falls precipitously. "Charity," though, is declining; "change" is moving up; and if you are banking on "Making a Difference" making a difference in your search results, just don't launch it in July or December— both of which look like inescapable pits on the graph. (Thank you, Skyhorse Publishing, for launching this book in May!)

As a charitable organization, you should be aware of the words that are commonly searched in your geographic area. If you operate in various countries and want to receive donations from those countries (like Half the Sky Foundation, previously discussed), then you should familiarize yourself with the terms that local philanthropists and volunteers use.

If you're serious about tweaking this part of your organization's online presence, though, you should speak with an SEO expert.

A DEVICE FOR EVERY KIND OF GIVER

Consumer companies study the best way to deliver their products. Charities seldom consider the best way to carry their message or engage their audiences.[55] Usually they think of things through their own lingo and in their own space, but that's not the world we live in. Each of us hears the language that speaks to us, and each of us is most comfortable in our own "home" and space, wherever those might be.

Case in point in our online world: Anthropologie now has an iPad app (designed by Revel Touch)[56] that allows shoppers to create an outfit online. Of course, I had to try it for myself. It's fun, and it's like a video game that charges you big bucks at the end when you win. A single screen allows you to navigate different categories (top, pants, dress, shoes, bag, earrings) and swipe through five to seven choices in each, adding them to your "bag." Then you can go to your bag and see the array on the left-hand column and the price—what I put together totaled a cool $1,388—and then choose to check out or not. Reviewers and commenters like those on the "Retail Design

---

[55]This blindspot is the primary subject of Katya Andreson's book Robin Hood Marketing and is why the book, as much as the author criticizes it, is a must-read for charity officials.

[56]Also viewable on Revel Touch's website.

Diva" blog have noted how it's certainly desirable to shop like this sometimes rather than buy clothes in poor lighting and with long lines at the cashier. The lesson I learned from the exercise is that it gives the user a different and in some ways more pleasurable shopping experience. At least, it's an option. This has applications to online giving, which we'll touch on in a moment.

Why was the app created?

Revel Touch learned in a May 2011 Forrester Research report[57] that 60% of tablet users used their devices to purchase items. The report also found that tablet users are five to six times more likely to buy with their devices than are smartphone users, and nearly twice as likely as desktop or laptop computer shoppers! We know from business journals that shopping online on Christmas Day 2011 was up 16.4% year over year, with a 173% increase in dollars spent using mobile devices and 7% of all purchases made on an iPad.[58] Clearly, users are accustomed to (a) using their devices to make financial transactions, and (b) are growing more confident in making larger and larger transactions. The tablet may become a more familiar face in purchasing transactions. Revel Touch merely helped Anthropologie go to where the customer is: sitting comfortably on her sofa in cotton pajamas and drinking coffee.

Yet, there were drawbacks with the app: users complained that it was difficult to click on what they wanted, and some

---

[57]BizRate/Forrester Research.
[58]http://www.bizjournals.com/louisville/blog/morning_call/2011/12/online-shopping-rose-164-percent-on.html

tablets (at least iPads) don't support Flash technology the way many PCs do. (Steve Jobs wrote in 2010 about Flash.[59] One of the reasons that Apple products don't support it is that, he claimed, Flash was developed by Adobe for using your mouse to rollover the video, etc., but not designed with touch functionality in mind.)

Are you delivering your message in a way that a donor can engage with and experience to the point of wanting to take action? And are you giving your donors multiple ways to engage? Different devices can translate into different donation revenue results.

The standout of course is Apple and its devices. Apple products have been proven through webcam eye-tracking studies to hold people's attention longer than other manufacturers' devices.[60] Many of us love the beauty in Apple products; it's hard not to stare. This means that if your apps, videos, messages, or appeals are *not* designed specifically with Apple in mind (if you're relying too much on Flash technology), you might be less effective than you could be in reaching your donors.

So now, in the era of consumerism, user experience, and glossy interfaces, charities must be aware of how their messages are coming across. Again, my recommendation is to avoid "marketing" as a core strategy, but rather to be aware of and use the available technology to invite givers into your vision for a better world. Making your message work on

---

[59]http://www.apple.com/hotnews/thoughts-on-flash/
[60]Forbes, Oct 28, 2011 http://www.forbes.com/sites/elizabethwoyke/2011/10/28/eye-tracking Heat maps show that the eye stays longer on iPhones and iPads than on their class competition.

the devices people are using, particularly Apple devices (with all their advantages and limitations), will enhance your effectiveness.

We've just covered the use of tablets, and using our laptop or desktop for financial transactions is the subject of this entire book, so we won't elaborate more here. We started out the book with a fictional episode around the very real Haiti earthquake that involved mobile giving, so let's take a slightly longer look at cellphones.

While giving from your cellphone is correctly considered "mobile giving" and not "online giving," since one can give via text while not on the Internet, it's often lumped in with online giving because it's electronic. Gifts via text are easy (no payment steps needed), allow for a low monetary commitment of even US $5 using an approved "Application Service Provider" (Connect2Give, mGood, etc.) that works with your cellphone provider, and boot off our charitable impulse and sense of human dignity, so they are most prevalent during disasters and crises. In early 2010, Haiti was hit with a 7.1 magnitude earthquake, and the death toll according to officials was 230,000. As others did in their own way, American Red Cross workers appeared in the news and asked the public to use their phones to text "HAITI" to "90999" (this is no longer an extant campaign), and $5 or $10 would be added to their phone bills. The Red Cross alone received $32 million from more than 3 million people making $10 donations.[61] This campaign by the Red Cross was such a success that in the annual survey of 2010 charitable giving by GivingUSA, released in June 2011, leaders had to asterisk their remarks

---

[61]Source: Convio. Online marketing benchmark study, March 2011.

in explaining the anomaly of giving to the international relief category. Similar remarks are made after statistics are skewed because of gifts following the Japan tsunami, the Indian Ocean tsunami, or Hurricane Katrina. This is a testimony to the generosity of global citizens and quick-acting agencies that work at scale that have also harnessed the power of the Internet and are pushing the boundaries. (Also, given this sector's history of normal ups and downs in yearly giving, it underscores the difficulty in sustaining an ever-increasing donation total outside of responding to disasters.)

Interviewed by *USA Today* in early 2011, the leader of the Mobile Giving Foundation said, "The best mobile giving campaigns are the ones where it's easy for consumers to donate, where the price points of entry are low, and where it's transparent how the funds are being used."[62] Additionally, Canadian givers are able to have 100% of donations "pass-though" to the charity, and by the time this book is printed, perhaps the same will be true in the U.S. (Carriers supporting the mobile giving platform include Verizon Wireless, AT&T Mobility, T-Mobile, Sprint/Nextel, U.S. Cellular, Cricket Communications, Cincinnati Bell and Cellular South.) Various studies have indicated that many people would give more via text if they could, some say up to $100.

With mobile giving, we're not talking only about adults with cellphones who can give money. We're also talking about teenagers under the age of 18 who may not be financial backers but who have this technology and can be encouraged to volunteer time or share links. For this audience, it's about the

---

[62] USA Today online. Feb 10, 2011. http://yourlife.usatoday.com/mind-soul/doing-good/kindness/post/2011/ 02/haiti-earthquake-taught-world

mobile *channel* as much as the device itself and leveraging that channel for charitable activity.

Aria Finger of DoSomething.org (whose mission is "using the power of *online* to get teens to do something good *offline*") helps lead an organization that harnesses mobile technology and goodwill among teenagers. She reminds us that while 75% of teens have cellphones, 72% have text-only capability. Only a minority, 33%, have smartphones and can surf the web. Engaging via text can reach all 75% that have a cellphone. And charities that have their constituents' cellphone numbers truly have dedication and loyalty, she says. (Many of us have email accounts for newsletter subscriptions we don't care about, so giving out our email address is less of a commitment.) DoSomething, on the other hand, conducts text campaigns and has some remarkable results. One campaign they ran with teenagers got a 20% response in nine minutes.[63]

Therefore, whether one is giving money or time, a campaign harnessing cellphone technology can be adapted by those organizations needing to raise money quickly during a crisis or motivate a committed core to take a small action.

THE DOS AND DON'TS

The Dos:

• **Make the site secure.** With online giving, there's little else that can top this.

---

[63]Statistics and opinions expressed at the NextGen:charity conference in NYC, 2011.

- **With restraint, offer incentives** (but see the don'ts below). Branded, logical incentives to reward those who give money or share a link with peers can be good community building. Run rampant and you get into unsustainable costs, you diminish your brand, and your donors will get angry.

- **Make it easy to give.** This means offer a variety of options with minimum clicks and on a web page that's been designed for easy navigation.

- **Make it fun to give.** Crowdrise does a good job with this— you never know what's going to come from them next. But remember: when dealing with our money, which is a serious topic, you have to add levity at appropriate times.

- **Your giving site should be aesthetically pleasing.** Of course, it needs to be branded in alignment with your overall site and nonprofit, but remember that people are used to making financial transactions in a secure but pleasing environment. There are some standards about the layout of a page with respect to giving that are covered well in a paper by interactive architect Heidi Adkisson and found on her website.[64] For instance, Adkisson found that all 75 of the sites with a "Shopping Cart" function (that icon showing that you have purchases or donations in progress) had a "global View Cart function," meaning the user can easily navigate to their financial transaction from any page or sub-page of the site. Additionally, she found that most sites positioned the icon for the Shopping Cart at the top of the page and right-of-center. Her paper is downloadable and is well worth referring to.

---

[64]http://www.hpadkisson.com/index.html

- **Having your giving page go viral is great, but not essential.** While not everyone can be charity: water, most nonprofits can find something for people to share, which might lead others back to the site or might not. Perhaps it's just something of added value that your supporters will continue to send to their friends to spread goodwill.

- **Build community.** Closely akin to the point above, and while the act of giving is very personal (and confidential in many cases), you want to find ways to enlarge your community through the giving process. Some sites offer a way to tweet announcements or events or to share them on Facebook, encouraging others to do likewise. Sometimes there's a link on the page itself or in the confirmation page or email confirmation that has a link you can share. Giving people the option to share peer-to-peer capitalizes on what they already like to do—tell someone something they're excited about and want that person to be a part of as well.

- **Encourage your givers.** Think of them like they're runners in a marathon and you're cheering them on from the sidelines. They are part of the team! We can do this thing together! Don't be overly smarmy and don't be insincere, but let your belief and enthusiasm in your cause show. Merely stating the need and crying poor-mouth is a sure buzz kill. Keep it upbeat and optimistic. You're in this line of work because you have hope, so let that be evident.

- **Make it "addictive" in the best sense.** I've already given to one of my favorite charities twice this month (it's year-end as I write), and I may give again. They use rotating banners which lead to different and interesting appeal letters, and I am constantly intrigued by what I'll find behind Door

#2. I enjoy seeing what pops up, and even if I only read the letter and nothing else, they've renewed my support, because they never cease to find ways to engage me. They care about me as a community member, so they give me new and inspiring content.

- **Evaluate and build your email list.** Acquisition of new members of your community is a lot cheaper these days than when one had to find them through direct mail (where there was a net loss of money in most cases). Remember also that your email list is not as good as you think it is. Email addresses change, and many people sign up with their junk addresses. If you can acquire cellphone numbers, this is perhaps the biggest information commitment a supporter can make, and it allows you to send text alerts to them. Use very judiciously. And go to DoSomething.org to learn some of their best practices.

- **Find partners to help exponentially leverage your message.** Our firm was creating a partnership to get a nonprofit's message out using a music video. The criteria for the nonprofit and the artist were that each partner needed to have an audience of a certain size that could be exposed to each other, presenting a win-win. (For v2.0, we will find a corporate partner to finance this with a 15-second ad up front.) The musician had fans across multiple social media platforms (Facebook, Twitter, YouTube, MySpace, her own website, and a mailing list), and the nonprofit had a mailing list along with mailing lists for their strategic partners that worked in-country (Africa) with them. We housed the video on the musician's YouTube channel but made a Facebook tab on the charity's page, so that all the traffic would come there but page views would register on the originating URL. Organizations like GoodScout[65] are finding these kinds of partnerships among artist, nonprofit and businesses.

- **Know your audience and when it reads its emails.** Convio and Blackbaud (among others) have white papers outlining which days and times of day people open emails, or look at links and videos. Email services like MailChimp and others can also stagger the sending of large email campaigns so that all messages hit at 9:00 a.m. on Tuesday in multiple time zones, all in local time.

- **Be aware of cultural differences, and believe what people tell you. <u>Listen</u>.** We've already seen that different words related to "donation" and "development" and "fundraising" and "scheme" are interpreted differently. If you have a diverse audience, consider the language you use and the posture you use if the ages of your supporters differ widely or if you work across national or linguistic lines. If you're doing microfundraising and hear from some of your friends to "back off" a bit, then heed their advice. If you have donors who want you to unsubscribe them, do it immediately, and notify them graciously that you've done so.

- **Be ok with failure.** On the artists' funding platform Kickstarter, there is a 43% failure rate. Fundraising is inherently entrepreneurial, which is inherently risky, and while good stewardship (read: conservation, management) is essential, so is finding new supporters and pioneering new forms of engagement. Don't be afraid to fail and to learn from it. If you're a manager at a nonprofit and you

---

[65]http://goodscoutgroup.com/

oversee someone who is responsible for online giving, part of your role is to set aside some budget for "smart failure."

- **Raise money in alignment with your ethos,** even if the experts tell you you're crazy. The strategy, techniques, giving page, and language all have to "feel" like you. This is a corollary to knowing your audience, for while it has to "feel" like you, your fundraising also has to appear seamless to your audience. No one wants to be sold, but most of us like buying. And we'll buy but only if we know it's *you* who's asking us, not a slick vendor whose web tool is designed to extract maximum dollars.

- **Make sure to THANK your donors after their gifts.** Multiple times. And send a report outlining how the money was spent.

The Don'ts:

- **Don't make tangible incentives the motivating factor behind a donor's gift.** (But see the DO's also). I received an appeal from a group, and they had placed an incentive as the third of three reasons why I needed to donate before year-end, which makes it the most emphatic. In fact, the incentive—a chance to win an iPad2—seemed to diminish who they were. It had the feel of a raffle, instead of a cause. Years ago, in a moment of obtuseness while I was watching public television and its annual appeal, I turned to my wife and said, "We should make a donation of $50 so I can get a new tote bag." She turned to me and—with a look that was trying to determine whether I was half asleep or half-brained—said, "Why don't you just buy a new tote bag for $10?" (I am convinced I was half asleep...)

Similarly, incentivizing people to give before year-end so they "can take a tax deduction" is all right, since that's actually helpful information, but most donors don't itemize on their tax returns anyway. Our recommendation is that if you must add incentives, brand them around your vision and send them after a gift, as a surprise thank-you. This might seem like a no-brainer (who doesn't want their brand traveling around as free advertising?). But it's a page from the playbook of visual merchandising.

Luxury merchandisers know that when people come into a high-end store, they don't want to commit yet to spending too much, and they don't always want to interact with a salesperson. Therefore, at the front of the store, usually to the right, are some of the branded fobs and trinkets (key chains with the company logo, for example), along with lower-priced items such as leather goods, perfume or body lotions. This allows browsers truly to browse, un-accosted, and to pick up an item at a low price point that gives them "the brand experience" and is aspirational. It draws them in closer to the higher-ticket items. Likewise, nonprofits might find ways to offer lower-priced incentives that are branded and which can be aspirational, drawing the donor deeper into the vision of the organization. And make the incentive connected with the program work on a common-sense level, like a branded mousepad from a group that helps schools get technology, or a branded coffee mug from a soup kitchen.

Incentivizing can introduce recurring costs; undermine donor loyalty, which may suffer because they hear about those costs or they stop giving when the tote bags disappear; and, arguably, incentives take away from the culture of philanthropy. If instead you say thanks with a token that the donor didn't expect (as opposed to ask them to give because of the token), many people appreciate the gesture.

- **Don't mistake community building for fundraising.** A small nonprofit, like a community or school group, says at a leaders' meeting, "We need to raise money!" So it embarks on what they think is a fundraising venture and in the process they do more community building and they miss the more efficient ways to raise money. Various fundraising programs that ask kids and adults to sell a basic item in bulk (usually foods like pizza, cookies, candy) and get some of the profits are better understood as community builders. Even one of the most popular national food fundraising companies that people sign up for online and then have their friends go online to make food reservations touts that one of its items can net a group "up to 50% profit." In the real world of fundraising, this is an extremely high cost of raising a dollar, and it takes no more effort to get 75% or 90% profit as it does 50% profit as long as you have the right fundraising model and strategy. Yet, these pizza "fundraisers" are great community builders, because it involves teams, a shared goal, and some kind of celebration at the end. It also can involve kids, whose parents are always looking for them to do something constructive and group-oriented. Public school PTAs are notorious for having dozens of "fundraisers" that often net what is considered a poor outcome in professional fundraising, but these activities all taken together are invaluable to build the community that will ultimately help meet the PTA budget and have a lot of fun doing so. If you employ these kinds of programs, you should be aware of how the numbers usually wind up.

- **Don't forget to consider supporting your campaign in real life.** The (RED) Campaign is an effort that many of us heard about or continue to via the Internet. Yet it relies on our regular shopping activity. As its site explains, each time you go into a Gap, for instance, and buy a (PRODUCT)^{RED}, part of the profits go to the cause. When you buy into an iconic brand like the Gap or Starbucks or now Coca-Cola, you are also buying into the (RED) brand, and vice-versa. This is another example of a nonprofit cause going to where the consumer is, and in some cases the businesses are almost subservient to (RED), so kudos to them.

THE THREE ATTRIBUTES OF MAJOR DONORS

From the very tactical to the broader, strategic part of fundraising, we're going to look at how to identify "major donors." Many people who support organizations are making larger and larger gifts online, and many mid- and upper-level givers to an organization will first check a site before making an online or offline gift, according to Convio. So we should understand who they are, and how they relate to your organization and the world of philanthropy.

Fundraisers know that givers of large donations tend to share at least two of these three attributes:

- **They have some kind of affinity with your organization.** They are an alumnus, former patient, or relative of someone directly and positively affected by your work.

- **They have a history of giving.** They have made philanthropic gifts before, even if not to your organization. They tend to give not just for the tax benefits but because they are "mission-minded." They care about your group's vision and they generally will continue to give so long as you follow that vision, they have the means to give, and you steward their gifts well.

• **They have capacity to give.** Even if they share the first two attributes but don't have capacity, they won't be making a large gift to your organization until they regain their capacity.

Let's take each attribute in its turn, starting with affinity.

It's hard to believe that eating a dried-out hamburger in a college dormitory cafeteria can translate to a major gift decades later. Yet, post-secondary institutions that create memorable experiences also create lasting relationships and communities, which are the basis of charitable giving. In fact, two famous universities only an hour apart experience levels of alumni giving very differently: one has 45% participation, and the other has 9%. The former has a campus that is removed from distractions (which allows the school experience to dominate the memory); the latter is in a large metropolitan area where the university, with no real campus center, has to compete for attention with exciting cultural and social offerings. Likewise, NYU's Stern School of Business sent to their alumni a comparison of peer institutions' percentage of alumni giving. Harvard had more than 25% of its alumni giving; Darden School of Business (UVA), more than 40%; Yale topped the list at 45%+. Stern was at 10% and ranked last on their own list. (Presumably, the school's Dean was trying to offer this data as a call-to-arms. I did not find the report or the letter encouraging, but perhaps the alumni did.) Interestingly, NYU omitted its neighboring peer to the north, Columbia (whose alumni giving is 15%[66]).

IRL (In Real Life): Columbia Business School's Worldwide Community

Columbia Business School wrote the following on its website: "During the 2010–11 fiscal year, the Office of Alumni Relations and its 60 volunteer-led alumni clubs hosted 332 events worldwide. This included Reunion 2011, which boasted a record-breaking attendance of nearly 2,200 alumni and guests. The fifth annual Worldwide Alumni Club Event took place in 58 cities around the world and was attended by more than 2,000 alumni, current students, and admitted students."

If I was an alumnus who read this, I'd be encouraged to give because of the robust activity my peers showed in getting together. And if I didn't attend one of those gatherings, I'd be more eager to set aside time on my calendar next year for it. Whether I make my gift online or off, the community at Columbia has made itself readily available for connections throughout the year and wherever I'm working.

While these are schools with budgets that perhaps far exceed your organization's, the principle is the same: a strong *community* fosters regular giving that can last a lifetime. Where can you find people who have affinity with your nonprofit and how can you strengthen their loyalty?

---

[66]http://www.businessweek.com/bschools/rankings/full_time_mba_profiles/columbia.html

Surprisingly, many organizations overlook their current donors to see who has the greatest affinity. For example, donors who give $250 or more each year for ten years in a row and are over the age of fifty-five should be contacted for possible planned gifts like annuities or bequests. Nonprofits should periodically screen their database for wealth indicators, no less frequently than every other year, perhaps more frequently with schools or membership organizations where the constituency is rapidly increasing in size and is transitory in job and residence.

Individuals aged thirty-five or younger who make a first-time financial gift of any amount have often volunteered first at that organization. Consider also that many younger people value their time more than their money, so when you engage them through voluntarism, they are investing a precious asset. Social media is a perfect way to do this. The more "face-time" you have with your younger volunteers via Facebook and Twitter, etc., and the more of their time they give—whether volunteering in person or using their social capital to share your organization's news and needs with their friends—the more likely they are to go "all in" and make a financial contribution.

There are times when nonprofits can go a bit over the top with fundraising. Ron Lieber wrote in the New York Times[67] how some organizations can take "prospect research" a bit too far. One thinks about an elderly rich person being admitted to a hospital and the development office paying a special visit to the private room, making sure there are fresh flowers

---

[67]NYT, Dec 16, 2011. http://www.nytimes.com/2011/12/17/your-money/fund-raising-taken-to-a-new-level- your-money.html?pagewanted=all&src= ISMR_AP_LI_LST_FB

or a comfy pillow. Learning about a donor's charitable giving capacity can influence the level of service. Likewise, we can overlook donors who come across very humbly and don't flaunt their wealth. Yet, there is certainly a time and place for approaching someone who has the ability to give. Hospitals do and should ask their wealthy clientele to help support their ongoing work. Schools do it. Churches do it. Zoos do it. Communities get stronger—it's our premise—when all members pull together to offer all their gifts, financial and otherwise, to advancing the common good.

While some organizations serve wealthy constituents, others serve poor ones who have no capacity to give (either time or money). Many of those same organizations indirectly serve surrounding neighborhoods and increase those neighborhoods' vitality in the course of carrying out their missions. Do the local residents know of your work? We are working with a client who has served a wealthy area for four decades, yet residents are all but ignorant to their existence. We believe that area citizens will appreciate this client's work and want to continue its service, because it makes the neighborhood more livable in addition to meeting a real human need.

Or take the example of New York's High Line. In late 2001, an order was signed to demolish this unused and rusted elevated railway, which once brought goods into the meatpacking district and Industrial West Side, and mail to the Post Office. Ten years later, it boasts the same visitorship as the Empire State Building. It's considered a must-see for any out-of-towner. All of Manhattan and even New York's other boroughs are served by the High Line in its accessibility and sheer beauty, and the city's donors see that and support it accordingly.

These are real-life examples rather than virtual ones, but what they point to is that you should marshal all connections your organization has with external constituents, going two or three levels deep.

- Do you have alumni?

- Have you provided services to affluent individuals?

- Have you helped a neighborhood where local residents would like to express their gratitude for your work?

- Who's on your newsletter mailing list?

- Do you have any white papers online that can be downloaded and thereby build an email list to write to occasionally?

- Have you approached your vendors?

- Do you have a gift shop or other auxiliary revenue lines that allow you to know a constituent's email address?

- Do you have followers on social media like Facebook, Twitter, or check-ins through FourSquare? How about commenters on your YouTube channel?

In addition to affinity, donors should have a history of philanthropic activity.

A lot of this is common sense. We all know people about whom we can say, "She's just a very giving person," right?

Just as some people are naturally gifted in singing, leadership, or tennis, some also are naturally gifted in giving generously to others. Many naturally generous people are good listeners, have a great deal of mercy, are empathic without losing judiciousness, unselfish, frugal, and are often analytical and insightful about an organization's finances and strategic planning. And we're not talking about only hedge fund owners; it might be your aging grandmother who spent her whole life living on a modest income but has become a master at budgeting and wants to look at the organization's P&L.

Organizations should seek to enhance their donors' understanding of and work in philanthropy, even if much of that increase doesn't go noticeably to the organization itself. The best development officers I know do this—they are not salesmen looking for the transaction; they are vision-casting surrogates for their employer and are also advocates for a donor's lifestyle of philanthropy. As you would coach the gifted tenor to hone that ability so that he could one day sing at the Met, so you should encourage the generous person to learn more about charitable giving for her own joy, and for the benefit of many, and not just to prompt her to give more to your organization. Community-based organizations such as the Silicon Valley Community Foundation and the Korean American Community Foundation have mission statements that refer to being generous givers and developing cultures of generosity, advancing the common good, and fostering greater civic participation. Of course, this is their essence—to give gifts—so it's more natural.

But what about your own nonprofit, which has to seek funds directly and meet its annual budget? One option is to recommend to your key givers that they find a philanthropic coach or advisor, and make it clear that your motivation is in their best interest, not yours. If you're a donor, searching for "philanthropy advisor" on the Web will produce a mixed bag, of course, and if you're affluent, you may have already considered starting a family office, but you should check with your local community foundation on resources. For donors to nonprofits in the religion sector, a group called Generous Giving hosts events found to be both spiritually transformative and also have greatly increased actual giving percentage among participants. At these events there's no fundraising allowed. The entire experience, whether at a three-day conference or a single day boutique event, is designed *for the givers*. It is to enrich them.

The alternative to enriching your donors is burning them out through solicitations (although there is a risk of overdoing stewardship and thanks and thereby exhaust them through too-frequent contact). Many givers who are repeatedly asked to give without being taught and coached about their own gift of philanthropy are like fields that farmers never let lie fallow—the topsoil washes away, they become useless and stop bearing fruit. So be true to your organization and wise about future sustainability. Grow your givers for *their* sakes.

After the above, it will seem very clinical discussing our third attribute of a major donor, but there's no way around it— major donors have to have capacity to make a major gift. If a donor has a very real affinity with your organization and has a history of giving but does not have capacity, then it's simple math that he won't be making a big gift.

We often ask ourselves, "Don't my wealthy donors have money to give?"

Maybe. But maybe not.

According to the Federal Reserve Bank, the average household debt-to-income ratio reached an all-time high of 133% in 2007, meaning the average family owes 33% more than they have in disposable income. (This figure is still at 115%.)

So, what should you look for in givers who still have something to give? Here are three types of appreciating assets, and each can be found online, albeit with some hunting:

First, see if they own real estate, using certain online tools that can determine the purchase price versus the assessed value.[68] Additionally, you can often determine what income level is needed to maintain the donor's properties.

See if they have insider stock positions. These are officers and directors who make policy at publicly-traded companies. Other insiders include those who own 10% or more of the company's stock. Insiders' activities regarding this stock is publicly available through SEC filings. Donating stock helps individuals avoid capital gains tax. Note: if your organization's website doesn't have information on how donors can donate stock, just include the following details on your giving page. The following is stock language you can alter for use on your website, and it contains basic elements donors look for:

> You can donate appreciated securities—stock, mutual funds, bonds, ADRs (American Depository Receipts), and other 'property'—and oftentimes receive a greater tax benefit than you would receive as compared to selling the appreciated securities and

---

[68]WealthEngine and Blackbaud's Target Analytics are two tools top fundraisers use.

then donating cash. Donations of appreciated securities are recorded as a charitable gift at the appreciated amount. Also, by donating appreciated securities you can avoid recording a capital gain in the security (assuming the investment has appreciated and that you have held the asset for more than one year). You should check with a tax professional before initiating any transfer of securities. If you would like to donate securities, you can initiate the transfer through your broker and request that the securities be transferred to:

Account Name: *"Organization Name"*
Account Number: *[brokerage account number]*
DTC #: *["Depository Trust Company" number;*
    four digits, obtained from broker or
    your CFO]

You should remind your donors when giving stock that they should be sure to have their names clearly indicated on transmittal forms. Brokerage firms sometimes transmit gifts without donor identity information and the nonprofit has to then hunt for similar stock gifts that might inform them of who made this latest gift. There is no way to donate stock online, per se, but your donors should be able to read about this option on your website.

The third appreciating asset is that your donor owns a business. Additionally, some business owners may want to learn about the "Charitable Shareholder" tool offered by at least one independent foundation.[69] In this model, the business owner

---

[69]The National Christian Foundation in Atlanta, and its affiliates around the country, is one example.

donates a non-voting interest in the business (which provides cash flow of profits to a nonprofit), gets a substantial tax deduction, and still maintains management oversight of the business without a reduction in lifestyle. Again, this option, along with others like real estate and stock, cannot be transacted online, but you want your website to outline all the possible options. Recall Convio's report that as many as 49% of first-time mid- and upper-level donors will first check your site before making a gift online or offline. They are doing due diligence, mainly, but if they see a way to give that is more advantageous to them tax-wise, then you've helped both them and your organization. So make sure your giving/donations page is comprehensive about options and current with charitable tax law.

THE NINE TESTS OF A HEALTHY NONPROFIT

There are now as many as 1.5 million charities to give money to. At last count, CrowdSourcing.org lists 1,547 different "niche crowd funding" sites, meaning there are almost 1,600 ways on the web alone (not even counting mail, phone or mobile device) to give to literally millions of organizations.

About now, we each start hyperventilating. Is it any wonder the donor is often cautious about how she makes that commitment to give?

How do we make sense of it? Here are some development-related or financial indicators to look for and some actions you can take before making a large donation or asking your friends to.

How Many Lapsed Donors Does the Organization Have?

In the private sector, a company thrives on repeat business from satisfied customers. Likewise with nonprofits, which should be able to count a high percentage of donors who continue to give each year as they see their gifts being used well, and who feel that they have been stewarded well. For first-time givers, a 70% retention rate is good. For donors who have given more than once, you would want to see a nonprofit keeping 90% of them. Web-based companies like Amazon, aggregating services like Travelocity, and especially user-review sites like Yelp have candid responses about service levels and product quality. While not scientific (the most unhappy people with free time are the most vocal online), it does allow for a more transparent purchasing experience. Your charity's development office should be able to let you know whether their donors are staying faithful to the mission by continuing to renew their giving each year.

Does the Nonprofit Receive Funds from Sustainable Sources?

87% of giving in the U.S. is done by individuals (either while living or through their estates). Some organizations, however, rely too heavily on government grants that change with administrations; on corporate money, which retreats in recessions; on foundations, which decrease grants when their endowments dip; or even on aging board members who have been over-tapped. San Francisco-based CompassPoint Nonprofit Services conducted an academy for nonprofits that relied heavily on government and foundation grants. They reported that 80% of participants were gaining more gifts from individual donors. Their academy workshops were based on the idea of grassroots fundraising, which is another way to understand online community building and fundraising.

Each nonprofit needs to have a right mix of sectors giving to them in a sustainable way. Make sure that the organization you want to give to is not about to plunge into the red next fiscal year because of over-reliance on a disappearing grantor or sector. For example, here in New York many day care centers rely almost solely on city and state funding. When that funding dried up due to priority budget initiatives in the face of decreasing federal block grants, those day care centers were left with very little revenue. They lacked individuals locally or near their neighborhoods who had vision and means to continue supporting them. They lacked foundation or corporate support. Your nonprofit may not accept government money as a policy, but that's not the issue. The question your organization needs to pose is whether or not you are "diversified" in the right ways. If you're a donor and want to learn about a nonprofit's reliance on government grants, you can check on their IRS Form 990.

The 2011 Giving USA report (most recent available and covering philanthropy in 2010), researched and written annually by The Center on Philanthropy at Indiana University, reported that the $291 billion in charitable contributions in this country was broken down as follows:

- Bequests – 8%

- Foundations – 14%

- Corporations – 5%

- Individuals – 77%

People like you and me, therefore, while we're living or as we plan upon our deaths, account for 85 cents of every dollar given to charity. Further, some foundation gifts are actually individuals giving through a family foundation or community foundation and misreported. Corporation gifts are often special event table purchases or sponsorships decided on by an individual who may be the company founder or principal. It's a truism to say that it's always individuals giving to charity. Certainly, that's so. But when a committee is deciding on a gift, this becomes more time-consuming for the organization, more expensive to steward, and is less sustainable. In your online giving and online fundraising, you are reaching out to individuals, even if it's in terms of one-time $10, $25, and $100 gifts, the very people who will form the donation spine of the organization for years to come. In this sense, online giving and its 3% contribution to your overall donation revenue total becomes much more of a player. Its role could be one of assists more than goals, but it's no less valuable.

To see where a nonprofit gets its gift revenue, you may have to ask the CFO for the P&L or Financial Statement. Many organizations will further break out the individual donation category into different constituent groups (e.g., schools might list board members, alumni, president's society, etc.).

Does Each Board Member Make a Yearly Donation to the Operating Budget?

Board health—and organizational health—is indicated by a board which supports staff leadership and takes its fiduciary responsibility seriously, including giving each year and to each campaign, and making the organization a top priority. (Some foundations won't even accept applications unless there is 100% board giving.) Board members also should be willing to discuss their estate plans with a professional in the development office or with the board chair.

This coin has two sides. An organization doesn't want its board to carry its revenue for too long, because that's unsustainable. However, it's remarkable to learn how many boards have poor giving participation. Some members forget. Some feel they do enough by coming to meetings or getting friends to give. I've even heard of some boards that have a majority of members who simply "don't want to do fundraising."

There's an old saying that your "heart follows your treasure." Read that again: it's not that you give your treasure where your heart leads you. We often find too many reasons not to give even at the brink of where we think our hearts will find fulfillment. Rather, our hearts follow our money. The treasure is like the engine, and the heart is the caboose. If I buy a thousand shares of a particular stock today, guess what ticker I'm calling up on Morningstar.com tomorrow morning and every morning that I own it?

When board members are presented with a written expectation to give and they fulfill this, their hearts will naturally follow, and that's good news for them and for the organization. They'll enjoy their board service more. You can ask the charity leader's office if they will release any documents outlining board roles and responsibilities and then ask how many board members follow any written expectation regarding fundraising.

Has the Nonprofit Stayed in the Black?

If it has finished the fiscal year with a deficit for three years in a row, that's a major red flag. Akin to that, how much debt does it have? Check the sites and tools listed below, because these figures are easily found online in the charity's Form 990. The yearly deficit or surplus is on the first page, Part I, Line 19. The net assets or fund balance listing is three rows down on Line 22.

Does the Organization's Development Office Have a Written Development Plan?

Capable staff leadership with the skills to create and execute a sound plan is vital to a healthy nonprofit. It's preferable that the head of fundraising be a CFRE or long-time development professional, rather than a recent transition hire from sales or financial planning, which provide some crossover skills but not nonprofit development management expertise.

Does the Board Have Both an Audit and Development Committee?

These are safeguards to make sure the organization is comprehensive and ethical on both the accounting and development sides. Call the organization and ask to speak to the executive director's assistant. While Sarbanes-Oxley (legislation enacted in 2002 to protect investors and bring greater accountability to public companies) was designed to be a watchdog and reform tool in the private sector, some of it has rubbed off in positive ways on nonprofits. As a donor, you should expect transparency and good stewardship, two qualities that Sarbanes-Oxley requirements have fostered in many nonprofit organizations.

Have you Reviewed the Charity Watchdog Sites?

Beyond GuideStar and BBB, you will want to check Charity Navigator and perhaps a start-up but very in-depth site called

Intelligent Philanthropy. (See Chapter 2, Section "For the Volunteer Fundraiser: Looking Under the Hood of a Charity's Financial Practices.")

Review the Organization's Form 990 for the Last Two or Three Years

We've referred to it a couple times previously, but it deserves its own section. Check revenue versus expenses, and how much the organization gets from donations versus other income. If it gets a lot of operating income from its endowment (you can see the total gain as "Investment income" in Part I, Line 10), that's a red flag. Often, this is great news for the non-profit, but sometimes it means the budget is overly dependent on endowment income and is not identifying new revenue sources. A drop in the stock market can mean massive staff layoffs and a failure to execute on program initiatives that were funded with donations. Also look at outside fundraising expenses, which are listed both in Part I, Line 16b and detailed on Schedule G, Part I.

Note: Two independent studies have found widespread inaccuracies on 990s, so if an organization's effectiveness or efficiency looks too good to be true, or if it looks abominable, have someone do extra due diligence.

Make a $100 Donation

See how the organization treats you. How quickly do they send you a receipt, and do they do so online? Do they thank you? Do they include a response device in their receipt mailing? For larger gifts or as a year-end summary, this is a good thing; it shows they are paying attention to repeat donations through the mail. See how you are stewarded after making a small donation. Do you feel valued?

When you give more wisely to the organizations that match your passion, and when you give through a method that is most advantageous to you and your family, you'll be a more cheerful giver.

5

What Happens When We Give: In Us and Around Us

Elsewhere in this book, you've read about Katya Andreson's encouragement to use corporate marketing's best practices to help bring your cause to the donor, using the private sector's marketing knowledge base. As I've said before, this is not inherently bad. For some givers, it provides a familiar and comfortable entry point that can lead them to a deeper practice of philanthropy and greater giving for the common good.

Still, other fundraising consultants have talked about how you as a fundraiser should approach givers the way people try to attract a romantic partner. One recently told nonprofit professionals gathered at a conference that instead of fundraisers persuading donors why they should give to the organization, they should *ask donors to explain why they would be good donors.*

"The best way to sell yourself is to have somebody else selling themselves to you," he said.[70]

There is a lot of truth to this, just as there is a lot of truth to what Andreson says. My point here, though, is that what is ultimately sustainable for both your organization and the donor is something different from both these approaches— something I'll argue is much more in line with the best parts of our human DNA and not so reliant on the expedient areas of our human psyche. It is what happens in us and around us that is, frankly, transformative and is also what will sustain giving to your organization. This sustainability requires that we understand who our real competition is, align ourselves with a vision, and follow our vocation. What will result is a stronger community.

WHO'S THE REAL COMPETITION?

Beneficiaries of a robust economy, Brazilians are flocking to Miami to buy luxury goods, which are less expensive in Florida than in South America. To accommodate them, many high-end stores are hiring Portuguese-speaking clerks who

---

[70]Chronicle of Philanthropy, December 13, 2011. http://philanthropy.com

can help fit the ladies into their Dolce & Gabbana dresses.[71] After all, why make it harder than it needs to be to buy? This is the essence of what retail merchandisers do—minimizing "excessive disruption." It's also what online fundraisers have been taught to do to be successful among the competition.

We've been taught incorrectly.

We in the nonprofit field often consider other nonprofits— whether in our sector or more broadly in the philanthropic world—the competition. Granted, donors do contrast one organization against another within sectors, and many donors have a certain amount they feel they can or want to donate each year. But the reality of what happens on an individual budget level is like what happens when we go out to a restaurant for a nice dinner. We look at the menu and then we tell the server our choice of one appetizer from among many and one entrée among many. Pretend you, the nonprofit, are one of those appetizers on the menu. You might start worrying about a different appetizer being chosen by the diner, when it's the entrée you need to worry about. Because what the patron is really there for is the entrée, not the appetizer, and if he's feeling a bit full, he's going to skip the appetizers.

So, who's the entrée?

Let's flesh this out in terms of the business schools we discussed earlier. Remember when NYU's Stern Business

---

[71]NewYorkTimes,December27,2011.http://www.nytimes.com/2011/12/28/ us/miami-courts-free-spending-brazilians.html?src=un&feedurl=http% 3A%2F%2Fjson8.nytimes.com%2Fpages%2Fnational%2Findex.jsonp

School sent a report to alumni comparing their giving to other business schools' alumni giving, hoping to motivate their base? The top performers were schools in New Haven and Charlottesville. Both those latter towns are nice to visit, but what they lack is world-class shopping, a big reason people come to New York and to NYU's campus. In addition to NYU students getting a great MBA, they are also awarded an honorary doctorate in spending money at New York's thousands of retail outlets. You can't help it here. So it's no wonder that residents anywhere—not just students at NYU or New York City residents—develop a masterful skill set in sniffing out the consumer opportunities around them. Katya Andreson knows this, and she's right!

The "entrée competition" we appetizer nonprofits face is not businesses that sell to us, though. Rather, we are the entrée. It's our desire to buy and own, and that desire is the opposite of charity. The best nonprofits (and if you want actual names, just look at a copy of the end-of-the-year *Chronicle of Philanthropy*) make us realize a vision of making someone's life better with no obvious tangible benefit.

Let's be real: When we get our paychecks, the first thing we think about is going out with friends, or paying a bill, or going shopping for pleasure—it's about our own wants and needs, right? Very understandable impulses. Charity, on the other hand, asks us to really consider that paycheck: "Does this first dollar go to me or to someone else?" Or, better put, "Is it conceivable that I could give this first dollar from my paycheck to someone else and keep the rest for myself?" Even that is countercultural and pretty radical. It's one of the better parts of our human DNA.

Here's how this makes a difference for online giving.

This individual uphill battle happens exponentially online, where it's scaled over millions of transactions. One can so easily surf between the Red Cross and Anthropologie and ESPN and Gmail, that even the best nonprofits will find it difficult to compete in the online space. We see the fight taking place even within the same arena. Consumers completing the final step of an online transaction can sometimes "round-up for Haiti relief," for example (where a consumer can round up their purchase to the next whole dollar amount and donate the difference to a nonprofit of their choice). It illustrates one small win in how this battle plays out. It's good to round up, certainly, but the thought, amount, and effort are equivalent to the tiny tip at the end of a meal.

And here's where nonprofits need to yield.

We can't and shouldn't fight the private sector—not offline, not rounding-up online, not anywhere. We'll lose.

We'll lose because we're fighting their battle—on their terms and on their turf. What we need is our own turf, an arena of vision, to which nonprofits should be calling their donors.

THE ARENA OF VISION

In its 2011 wrap-up, the *Chronicle of Philanthropy* listed the top buzzwords and phrases of the year. Starting with the Twitter hashtag (#), which isn't disappearing anytime soon, it also cited "disruption," saying the word "may soon replace innovation as the most overused and approaching meaningless term in philanthropy."[72]

That said, what does it actually mean?

As Lee Fox notes on CauseCapitalism.com, "Collectively, we spend billions of hours a year playing solitaire. So how can we capture that time to benefit the causes we want them to get behind?"[73] Taken from Harvard Business School professor Clayton Christiansen's idea of "disruptive innovation," this new term describes how a new population can participate in a way that was historically only accessible to an elite group.

IRL (In Real Life): Preserving literature

reCAPTCHA—This example is online, but it's too good to pass up as an illustration of disruptive philanthropy.

You probably have come across the "reCAPTCHA" tool when signing up for an online news source that you want to read but must register for first. There are two purposes to this process, which requires you to type in the letters of two words that appear warped and fuzzy. The first purpose is to ensure that you're not a robot.

The second, though, is a bit of disruptive philanthropy that the content provider is having you participate in.

While the provider's software knows one of the words and simply presents it to you to parrot it back, the second word is actually a scanned image from

---

[72]December 27, 2011. http://philanthropy
[73]http://causecapitalism.com/disruptive-philanthropy-from-the-social-enterprise-alliance-summit/

an older hard-copy edition of their own newspaper that they haven't identified yet. No computer has been able to decipher it, nor has any person taken the time to interpret the original. When you and others type in the word that corresponds to that scanned image, you are helping restore older newspaper content, and the provider, in offering you free news, is satisfying a philanthropic purpose in reclaiming all-but-lost content.

When I learned why reCAPTCHA does what it does (granted, it also saves the news provider time and money), I was glad to know that I had been interrupted so many times. It seemed worth the hassle.

The other side of the coin is how I shop. I joke with friends that when I go into a store looking for a dress shirt, I know exactly which shirt I want and usually where it is—Men's Department, white, Pinpoint Oxford cotton, French cuffs, 17 neck, 34 length. In and out as silently as possible, I'm like a U.S. Navy SEAL extracting a hostage from Macy's, and I want no excessive disruption. If you get in my way, I will take. you. out.

I'm completely in it for the shirt. But philanthropy, "disruptive" or otherwise, is actually *designed* to interrupt our busyness and ask us to take a look at what could be. Now let's rachet up the scale and increase the vision from one newspaper's content to a global knowledge base.

In his forward to Eve Blossom's book <u>Material Change</u>, designer Yves Behar notes that in business and particularly in branding, the idea of partnership between designer and client is extending outward to include the customer. "To influence how brands respond to and fit within important issues in the world," he writes, "designers and their clients need to collaborate."[74] This is where businesses and brands are learning from nonprofits, though they may not realize it. Those of us in development know that to make our annual budget, we go to our donors to ask for their renewed support. We often call them our "partners." We are accountable to them, so much so that a misuse of their donations is illegal. Donors almost always have opinions about how we run our programs. There has always been a close relationship in strong nonprofits between their staffs and their donors. The close relationship is built on and sustained by a shared vision.

Nonprofit professionals who want to raise a lot of money will ultimately have to give donors the opportunity to enter into a relationship with the organization that—through sharing expertise, appropriate levels of decision-making, and being granted accountability—allows for a transformative experience for everyone involved.

When you enter an Apple Store or an Anthropologie, for example, something visceral happens. You *feel* different. You actually *want* to buy something. There is a type of transformation that takes place, because what you feel is that somehow what you buy will make you different once you leave. You are catching a bit of the company's vision for *you* from buying their brand. Even the manikins and "look walls" that display completed outfits provide a quasi-"vision" of what we could look like if we buy the clothes that are displayed. Merchandisers point out that many of us feel insecure about putting an outfit together, so manikins and look walls do that

---

[74]page 6; Eve Blossom, <u>Material Change</u>, 2011, Metropolis Books, New York, 2011.

work for us. They give the imprimatur to our choices, so we ring up our purchase and walk out happy. Yet with all the "visions" of what might be in store for us when we visit an Anthropologie or Apple Store, we're fickle creatures when it comes to products. It's quite likely that at some point in our lives, a different computer company will come along with a better laptop. And when that happens, it's inevitable that many of us will switch to what's next.

Just like that.

The idea of a "vision" in the marketplace has long existed in the nonprofit sector. But when a nonprofit engages a donor at a level that only a nonprofit can, it's a different kind of transformation. The nonprofit speaks with the language of vision beyond the donor herself, the language of ideals. And deep down that's what people want, even if they never articulate it out loud. Those who do speak it do so in the most simple and elegant terms. A 25-year-old woman completes a walk-a-thon in Central Park to raise awareness about heart disease in women and afterwards is stopped by a television news reporter. The reporter asks her why she walked for so long in the rain and cold.

"I did it for Mom."

And we get it. We hear the story she hasn't told us in full and we resonate with the vision that she's referring to. We want to be part of that vision and those unchanging ideals, because that's a part of our human DNA. If you're a nonprofit leader, you have to allow your donors to engage with your vision as part of their own lives. It has to touch them in a way that transcends their daily living. Donors know this.

How does the idea of vision play out in your nonprofit? Let's say you're a child sponsorship organization, and through a donor's monthly online gifts and good stewardship, you allow her to feel apart of something greater than herself. It's a sense of justice that causes her to stop and consider, "No child should suffer like this. I am going to help this one boy." Or you're a breast cancer advocacy organization, and your donor— a construction worker—decides to make a monthly gift and wear a pink bracelet around the job site. He is driven by compassion, empathy, and love. His pals won't tease him, because they know his wife had a double mastectomy last year. He gives so that your organization can continue working to find a cure. He even tells his friends at the job to make sure their wives get mammograms. Some take pink bracelets from him.

Compassion. Love. Justice.

These are hefty ideals, and when your organization has them at its disposal, creating a vision might seem fairly straightforward.

But what about an organization where the main offering is screen after useful screen of black type and obscure information—about 3.8 million screens, to be exact. Wikipedia and the 501(c)(3) that runs it, the Wikimedia Foundation, have touched on something we all crave. They've accomplished it through community. Specifically, they have:

- Appealed to the *idea* of community

- Appealed directly *to* the community

- Asked the *community itself* to create their own appeals

At year-end, they run simple banner ads that take up about 1.5 inches of the top of your screen when you navigate to a Wikipedia page. You click through and read an appeal letter 3/4ths of a screen long and a request to give US$5 or more. Right under the giving box, they tell you where the donation will be used. Now that they have a few years' worth of experience, they've found several "appeal principles" to apply. One of them is that they tell their writers to stress, "Beauty. Wikipedia is an amazing, beautiful thing run by volunteers doing it out of the goodness of their hearts." And it is. It is like a colonial American commons, tended to by the local townspeople for the benefit of the group as a whole. As global citizens, you and I are the townspeople who are writing down, tweaking, and revising the world's knowledge-commons.

Beautiful.

Jay Walsh of Wikimedia said that while they experience great results from appeals written by the founder, Jimmy Wales, they also get surprisingly good results from appeals written by other members of the community—article contributors, donors, and staff. Walsh says they merely find their writers' passion about the project and then "get out of the way." Of course, appeals written by the wider community "require good editing and a package around the story. But it's almost like a journalistic process. We don't want to be too flashy. [Wikipedia users] expect the same simple, smart experience from the fundraising appeals" that they find on the site.

Because of the organization's scale, they can also run A/B tests on banners and letters and get results within hours.

As founder, "Jimmy always had in the back of his mind that [Wikipedia] would be a philanthropic project. So we created the Wikimedia Foundation. The first fundraiser we did was to raise money to buy our first tech staff member a laptop, because his was broken. The 'inner' community appealed to itself, and we raised a couple thousand dollars. The trend since then has been to talk to our readers and community."

Wikimedia doesn't even have the same boundaries separating parts of the non-staff community that other nonprofits might have. Donors and editors are both handled by a "Community Department." The development staff is nested within this department, as is the volunteer outreach team, which includes non-staff article contributors.

In early December 2009, Wales posted an appeal that brought in $430,000 from 13,000 people on the first day. By the close of the month, they had reached their $7.5 million goal.[75] "We get a vast number of small donations from all around the world," said Walsh. "We continue to talk to foundations, and they have come forward in making donations. But that's changed. We've moved to having everybody fund this. The average gift amount has gone down from $28 in 2010 to about $20 in 2011, and we see this as a good thing." They use GlobalCollect to accept a variety of currencies from more than 150 countries.

In Wikipedia's donation revenue model, the "townspeople" are being asked to take care of the commons, and they want you to see that you're a valued member of the town. The organization had less than 200,000 donors in 2008, but as of January 1, 2012 had topped a million. Each year when they

---

[75]Sources: ReadWriteWeb.com, Chronicle of Philanthropy, Huffington Post.

raise enough money to make budget, they stop fundraising and take down their banner ads.

The appeals themselves are rich in vision and personal story. They often read like one friend talking to another.

This selection is from a 2011 appeal by Wales, one of several they tested:

"Wikipedia is something special. It is like a library or a public park. It is like a temple for the mind. It is a place we can all go to think, to learn, to share our knowledge with others. It is a unique human project, the first of its kind in history. It is a humanitarian project to bring a free encyclopedia to every single person on the planet.

Every single person."

This letter paints familiar pictures—a library, a park, a temple. And it asks us to aspire to something that's not there yet. It has its own poetry in the repetition of the last line. As my mother said about beautiful writing, "It sings."

Or, here's the opening to an appeal written by Wikimedia Foundation programmer Brandon Harris that was among the most popular:

I feel like I'm living the first line of my obituary.

I don't think there will be anything else that I do in my life as important as what I do now for Wikipedia. We're not just building an encyclopedia; we're working to make people free. When we have access to free knowledge, we are better people. We understand the world is bigger than us, and we become infected with tolerance and understanding.

When you are invited to hear from someone who feels they're doing something worthy of a newspaper obituary or to be etched into a tombstone, you can't help but get caught up in the vision. With Wikipedia, enjoying 475 million unique visitors to the site every month—for free and with no advertising—it's no wonder there's strength in an appeal that ends with Wales saying, "Your donation will help keep Wikipedia free for the whole world."

OUR VOCATIONS AND THE COMMUNITY

Designers in Gary Hustwit's 2009 documentary, *Objectified*, talk about how objects prompt emotion. One designer noted how his job was to look into the future, using no frame of reference, and to design what was not there yet. In a sense, Wikipedia is doing just that. On its home page, a globe made of puzzle pieces remains unfinished. Each piece has a letter from a different language's alphabet on it. Each piece is different; each piece fits; each piece is necessary to complete the whole. Your contribution of an article or your contribution of a financial gift at year-end is necessary—they would claim—to get closer to finishing that picture of the world: where everyone has access to a free encyclopedia with the world's collective knowledge at our fingertips. They are the designers, but so are you! And your piece is essential! This is a vision that captivates a giver and doesn't require thousands of dollars of marketing, or branded fobs, or sexy videos. And more than one million people around the world have responded to Wikipedia's call.

There is a call—a vocation—that you've responded to in your current nonprofit role or in your current task of helping a nonprofit as a micro-fundraiser or giver. Perhaps you're still trying to determine what that vocation is, because that search is the third core part of our human DNA discussed here.

I was born in a big city, which I love, and yet I moved away and have returned now three times. I love this city's sounds, its smells and its people. Its shops, restaurants, sidewalks, subways, and skyscrapers. I love its materiality and tangibility. Yet the reason I returned the third time, with family in tow, was to answer a call, *my* call, my *vocation*. As much as I love this city, there are things missing. Those things are sometimes tangible, sometimes not (I'm sure many New Yorkers wonder what the next High Line will be). But they are things we first have to imagine and then find a way to make real. Some things are broken that we have to imagine are fixed. Some things are wrong that we have to imagine are made right. And some things are beautiful that we have to imagine are created. This is where nonprofits come in. And this is where philanthropy in general and online giving in particular comes in. While cities have historically formed around ports and grown from robust consumer trade, the Internet was founded around information and ideas.

Around vision.

Online giving must root itself in vision, because vision is the currency of the Internet as commercial trade is the currency of cities.

You, the online fundraiser or online giver, are participating in the next step in our global community evolution—from a disparate array of local cultures connected through the trade of disposable consumer goods to a durable fabric of business, philanthropy and charity—a community ready to fix, make right, and create. And this fabric is most visible in a surprisingly transparent platform—the Internet.

In Part One, we saw a woman in a coffee shop texting with her friend about the Haiti earthquake and making a small donation from her phone. One reason online efforts were so successful in early 2010 was certainly due to charitable responses on an individual level, but another reason was also because of the viral nature of global communities. We said this book's thesis was that, *"through charitable giving online, a united community creates and embodies change for the common good."* The young woman in the coffee shop, the couple in Houston, Tania Major in Queensland, the donors to Wikipedia from 150 countries—all are part of a growing philanthropic community embodying change for the common good.

If you want to have a successful online giving program, you first need to create the strong community in which that program can exist. You and your donors then need to understand who the competition really is and who it is not. Instead, your vocation answering the call is to engage with what *could be*, motivated by ideals that don't change. The result is a strengthened community, one that if bound by and kept strong in the same vision, will innovate ways to sustain itself and seek the common good.

We don't need another tote bag.

Appendices

On the following sheets users will find a compilation of research done by Zoey Creative Development and the HP Foundation. The purpose of the HP Foundation's research was to provide users a catalog of websites that would benefit a nonprofits fundraising, volunteering, and research efforts by showing what were some of the more visited sites that focused on enhancing the presence of organizations and causes in the nonprofit arena. Zoey Creative Development's purpose was to show in granular detail the differences between different "giving platforms" and "charity databases." The hope is that these findings will help both casual and institutional fundraisers better assess the resources that are at their disposal and in turn better target donors, raise more money, and better address the needs of their cause. With this information users will be able to make side by side comparisons and see which sites best address their and their constituents' needs.

Appendix A
List of Online Giving Platforms

Giving Platforms Section 1 (A)

Provider Name	Sample Nonprofit User	Ideal Organization Type	Web-site Design
actionatlas.org	*National Geographic*	large institutional	N
Amazon Payments	many	large institutional	Y
ammado.com	Nokia Siemens	variety	Y
ArtezInteractive.com	The Salvation Army	large and midsize institutional	Y
Authorize.net	many	large and midsize institutional	N
Avalon	University of Tennessee	large and midsize institutional	Y
Causes.com	His Father's Heart	micro-fundraisers, individual causes	N
CauseVox.com	Do it in a Dress	micro-fundraisers, individual causes	Y
changingthepresent.org	Alzheimer's Association	large and midsize institutional	N
Citizeneffect.org	1Well	micro-fundraisers	Y
Click and Pledge	many	large and midsize institutional	Y
Convio*	New York Public Library	large and midsize institutional	Y
Crowdrise	LA Food Bank	micro-fundraisers, individual causes	N

*As book was going to press, Blackbaud was in the process of acquiring Convio. Readers should confirm Convio's offering and fees directly with the company. Details here refer to the company's 'Common Ground' platform for small to mid-sized nonprofits. Its 'Luminate' platform is for larger nonprofits and is not detailed here.

Donor Communications	Social Media Integration	Web Analytics/ Reporting	Database Integration/ Management	Disbursement Frequency
N	None	N	N	Monthly
N	None	Y	Y	5–7 business days
Y	FB, T, IN, G	N	Y	Monthly
Y	FB, T, V, IN	Y	Y	Next day
N	N	N	Y	Next day
N	None	Y	Y	10–12 business days
N	FB	N	N	Monthly
Y	FB, T	Y	Y	Either real-time or weekly
Y	FB	N	Y	Monthly
N	FB, T, YT	N	N	Monthly
Y	FB, T	N	Y	Next day
Y	FB, T, IN, FLKR, YT	Y	Y	Next day
N	FB, T	N	N	Network for Good-monthly; Amazon-realtime

Facebook (FB), Twitter (T), YouTube (YT), LinkIn (IN), StumbleUpon (SU), Google (G), Vimeo (V)

Giving Platforms Section 1 (B)

Provider Name	Sample Nonprofit User	Ideal Organization Type	Web-site Design
DonorsChoose.org	Student Organizations	micro-fundraisers	Y
egive-usa.com	Churches	large institutional	Y
eTapestry.com	Northwest Children's Home	start-ups, and small to midsized nonprofits	Y
EverydayHero	ABC Fund	variety	Y
Firstgiving	Special Olympics-Illinois	micro-fundraisers, individual causes	Y
Givezooks!	The Moyer Foundation	micro-fundraisers, individual causes	N
Givology.org	Small organizations	micro-fundraisers, individual causes	N
globalgiving.com	Center for Wildlife	micro-fundraiser	Y
GoFundraise.com	Individuals	micro-fundraisers, individual causes	Y
Google Checkout	many	large institutional	N
greatergood.org	Greater New Orleans Foundation	variety	N
HelpAttack!	American Red Cross	micro-fundraisers, individual causes	N
jolkona.org	AXIS Dance Company	micro-fundraisers, individual causes	N

Donor Communications	Social Media Integration	Web Analytics/ Reporting	Database Integration/ Management	Disbursement Frequency
Y	FB, T	N	N	RealTime
N	FB, T, IN	N	Y	Weekly
Y	FB, T	Y	Y	Next day
Y	FB, T	Y	n/a	10–12 business days
Y	FB, T, YT	Y	N	Monthly
Y	FB, T	Y	Y	Next day
Y	None	N	Y	Next day
Y	FB, T	N	Y	Monthly
Y	FB, T, YT	Y	Y	10–12 business days
N	None	N	Y	10–12 business days
N	FB	N	N	Monthly
Y	FB, T	N	N	Monthly
Y	FB, T, YT	N	N	Quarterly; one-off pmts for disaster relief orgs

Facebook (FB), Twitter (T), YouTube (YT), LinkIn (IN), StumbleUpon (SU), Google (G), Vimeo (V)

Giving Platforms Section 1 (C)

Provider Name	Sample Nonprofit User	Ideal Organization Type	Web-site Design
Just Give	Hope Ethiopia	micro-fundraisers, individual causes	N
missionfish.org	University of Missouri	large institutional	N
modestneeds.com	Individuals	micro-fundraisers, individual causes	N
Network for Good/ Donate Now	Guidestar Registered Nonprofits	Small and growing nonprofits	Y
PayPal	Salvation Army	large and midsize institutional	N
Razoo	Society for the Arts in Healthcare	micro-fundraisers, individual causes	Y
SAGE	Habitat for Humanity Winnipeg	large and midsize institutional	Y
SeeYourImpact.org	Door of Hope	micro-fundraisers, individual causes	N
sixdegrees.org (see network for good)	Case Foundation	micro-fundraisers, individual causes	Y
socialactions.com	n/a	micro-fundraiser	N
Uend.org	Individuals	micro-fundraisers, individual causes	N
universalgiving.org	SEE Change	large institutional	N
YourCause.com	St. Jude Children's Research Hospital	variety	N

Donor Communications	Social Media Integration	Web Analytics/ Reporting	Database Integration/ Management	Disbursement Frequency
Y	FB	Y	N	Monthly
Y	FB, T	N	Y	Next day
N	FB, T	N	Y	Next day
Y	FB, T, IN, G, SU	Y	Y	Monthly
N	N	N	Y	RealTime
Y	FB, T	Y	N	Monthly
Y	FB, T, IN, YT	Y	Y	Next day
Y	FB, T	N	N	Monthly
Y	FB, T, IN, G, SU	Y	Y	Monthly
N	FB, T	N	N	RealTime
Y	FB, T	N	N	The following year
N	None	N	N	Next day
N	FB, T, IN	N	N	Monthly

Facebook (FB), Twitter (T), YouTube (YT), LinkIn (IN), StumbleUpon (SU), Google (G), Vimeo (V)

Giving Platforms Section 2 (A)

Provider name	Set-up Fee	Monthly Fee	Processing/Discount Rate
actionatlas.org	$0	$0	2–4%
Amazon Payments	$0	$0	1.9–2.9%
ammado.com	$0	$0	5–7.5%
ArtezInteractive.com	varies	varies	varies
Authorize.net	$99	$20	2.19%
Avalon	$0	$129–$499	0–2.5%
Causes.com	$0	$0	4.75%
CauseVox.com	$0	$39	varies
changingthepresent.org	$100	$0	3.00%
Citizeneffect.org	$0	$0	3.00%
Click and Pledge	$950/w Website Manager	$50	2.85–4.5% (eChecks 1.85%)
Convio	Contingent upon add-ons	$200–$425	Contingent upon adopted level
Crowdrise	$0	$0	3.99–5%

Transaction Fee	Payment Gateway	Recurring Gifts Accepted	CC's Accepted	eChecks, ACH or EFT Gifts
	n/a	Y	Amex, Disc, MC, V	Y
$0.30	Amazon Payments	Y	Amex, Disc, MC, V	Y
$0.00	WorldPay	Y	Amex, Disc, MC, V	Y
varies	Whoever the organization uses	Y	Depends on the organization's payment gateway	Y
$0.10	Authorize.Net	Y	Amex, Disc, MC, V	Y
n/a	Avalon	Y	Amex, Disc, MC, V	Y
$0.00	Network ForGood	Y	Amex, Disc, MC, V	N
$0.08	PayPal, FirstGiving, Stripe	Y	Amex, Disc, MC, V	N
$0.30	ImportantGifts, Inc.	Y	Amex, Disc, MC, V	N
$0.00	n/a	N	MC, V	N
$0.27–$.035	n/a	Y	Amex, Disc, MC, V	Y
	Pay Pal, Amazon Payments, bank transfers	Y	Amex, Disc, MC, V	Y
$1 for gifts under $25. $2.50 for donations of $25 or more	Amazon Pymts or Network for Good	N	Amex, MC, V	N

Giving Platforms Section 2 (B)

Provider name	Set-up Fee	Monthly Fee	Processing/Discount Rate
DonorsChoose.org	$0	$0	6.10%
egive-usa.com	$0	$10/$30	1.95–2.95%
eTapestry.com	$0	$99–$399	Contingent upon adopted level
EverydayHero	n/a	n/a	n/a
Firstgiving	$0	$300/year	7.50%
Givezooks!	$0	$129	2.20%
Givology.org	$0	$0	2–4%
globalgiving.com	$0	$0	15.00%
GoFundraise.com	$0	$20	4.95–6.93%
Google Checkout	$0	$0	1.9–2.9%
greatergood.org	$0	$0	0.00%
Help Attack!	$25	$0	8.25%
jolkona.org	$0	$0	2–4%

Transaction Fee	Payment Gateway	Recurring Gifts Accepted	CC's Accepted	eChecks, ACH or EFT Gifts
$0.00	Pay Pal	Y	Amex, Disc, MC, V	Y
0.2/$0.10	Sage Solutions	Y	MC, V	Y
	n/a		Amex, Disc, MC, V	Y
n/a	n/a	Y	Amex, MC, V	Y
$0.00	n/a	N	Amex, Disc, MC, V	N
$0.30	Sage, PayPal, Authorize.Net, Amazon Payments, Cyber Source	Y	Amex, Disc, MC, V	Y
$0.00	Google Checkout	Y	Amex, Disc, MC, V	Y
$0.00	PayPal	Y	Amex, Disc, MC, V	Y
$0.20	n/a	N	Amex, MC, V	N
$0.30	Google Checkout	Y	Amex, Disc, MC, V	Y
$0.00	n/a	N	Amex, Disc, MC, V	N
$0.00	First Giving	N	Amex, Disc, MC, V	N
$0.00	Google Checkout	Y	Amex, Disc, MC, V	Y

Giving Platforms Section 2 (C)

Provider name	Set-up Fee	Monthly Fee	Processing/Discount Rate
Just Give	$0	$0	4.50%
missionfish.org	$0	$0	2.20%
modestneeds.com	$0	$0	2.19%
Network for Good/ Donate Now	$199	$49.95/month	3% (fixed regardless of card)
PayPal	$0	$0	2.20%
Razoo	$0	$0	2.9% (extra 2% for team fundraising tools)
SAGE	$295	15 monthly, $50 annually	2.19% (Only for MC, V, and Disc)
SeeYourImpact.org	$0	$0	0.00%
sixdegrees.org (see network for good)	$0	$0	3% (fixed regardless of card)
socialactions.com	$0	$0	2.20%
Uend.org	$0	$0	0.00%
universalgiving.org	$0	$0	2.20%
YourCause.com	$0	$0	3% (fixed regardless of card)

Transaction Fee	Payment Gateway	Recurring Gifts Accepted	CC's Accepted	eChecks, ACH or EFT Gifts
$0.00	n/a	Y	Amex, Disc, MC, V	N
$0.30	PayPal	Y	Amex, Disc, MC, V	Y
$0.10	Authorize.Net	Y	MC, V	Y
$0.00	n/a**	Y	Amex, MC, V	N
$0.30	PayPal	Y	Amex, MC, V, Disc	Y
$0.00	US Bank	CC only	Amex, MC, V	N
$0.50	n/a	Y	Amex, MC, V, Disc	Y
$0.00	PayPal, Google Checkout	Y	Amex, MC, V, Disc	Y
$0.00	Network For Good	Y	Amex, MC, V	N
$0.30	PayPal	Y	Amex, Disc, MC, V	Y
$0.00	Donor Trust	Y	Amex, Disc, MC, V	N
$0.30	PayPal	Y	Amex, Disc, MC, V	Y
$0.00	Network For Good	Y	Amex, MC, V	N

**As back-office tools, Payment Gateways are often not evident.

Giving Platforms Section 3 (A)

Provider name	Pros
actionatlas.org	As a cause you have access to the same exposure as *National Geographic*.
Amazon Payments	Provides millions of Amazon.com customers with a convenient, familiar, and trusted payment experience on your site and helps optimize conversion.
ammado.com	Supports 76 currencies and languages.
ArtezInteractive.com	ArtezInteractive affords its customers a comprehensive suite of products that allows them to fully utilize an online presence.
Authorize.net	Authorize.Net has lower processing and transaction fees than some providers and they accept all major credit cards.
Avalon	Avalon is a global merchant provider that accepts all major credit cards and eChecks.
Causes.com	Walks you through the startup process step-by-step. No prior fundraising experience is needed.
CauseVox.com	Clean look and feel; low cost. Intuitive therefore good for micro-fundraisers who might be new to online giving. Good for smaller nonprofits and start-ups. Easy to design branded website.
changingthepresent.org	Cheap way to raise support.
Citizeneffect.org	You can easily engage your existing network of donors through Facebook, Twitter, and YouTube.
Click and Pledge	Flexible account plans.
Convio	Full portfolio of products, strong customer service, and nonprofit research sources.
Crowdrise	Similar to Facebook in that you create your own profile but with philanthropic info. Points are awarded that can be redeemed for prizes such as clothing, electronics, etc.

Cons
Only for *National Geographic* sponsored causes.
Does not provide access to social media.
Ammado does not provide any reporting services.
In addition to your payment gateway charging your organization a fee, Artez also charges a tranaction fee.
For a micro-fundraising effort Authorize.Net's fees might be a bit high, and for a more established organization they don't provide some of the value added services that other do.
Avalon is not integrated with any of the major social media sites.
Only accepts CCs and does not allow you access to your donors' information. Not a good source for someone starting off. Best used by people who have an established network.
Email notifications for gifts; no messaging as of December 2011.
Lacks the design edge that other provides have. They also doesn't accept FT/ACHs.
Limited on the credit cards and types of gifts that it can accept.
Not ideal for a micro-fundraiser.
Not condusive to smaller casual efforts.
Charity must be registered with Guidestar.

Giving Platforms Section 3 (B)

Provider name	Pros
DonorsChoose.org	Teachers can quickly raise funds for needed projects.
egive-usa.com	Easy setup for church and other nonprofits that need a EFT/ACH processing services.
eTapestry.com	Variety of price-points for different nonprofits. Solid company with proven customer service. Cloud computing.
EverydayHero	EverydayHero's payment processing system delivers funds straight to your organizations bank account.
Firstgiving	Provides nonprofits with fundraising management tools. Donors can choose to take on the transaction fees that are normally passed to the nonprofit.
Givezooks!	Very customizable and can process all major credit cards and EFTs.
Givology.org	Givology partners with leading grassroots nonprofit organizations, local communities, and schools to sponsor education grants and innovative community-based education projects.
globalgiving.com	Accepts a wide range of gifts, e.g., public and private stocks, checks, CCs. Donor gets follow up email regarding the use of their gift. Donors can get refunded with a voucher if they feel their gift was not properly used.
GoFundraise.com	Through GoFundraise donors can utilize their social networks to help promote the organization or cause of their choice through interactive and dynamic websites and emails.
Google Checkout	Donors can choice from a variety of payment options.
greatergood.org	Donors can purchase items and have a percentage of purchase go to a charity of their choice.
Help Attack!	With each update on Twitter or Facebook, you make a small donation to your cause. Gaming and discovery component.
jolkona.org	Donors have the luxury of using Google Checkout.

Cons
Only applies to licensed teachers.
Simply a online giving platform service. Does not offer any type of social media integration.
$1,188 per year for lowest-priced solution. Not cheap for a start-up nonprofit.
Not well known outside Australia.
Does not accept EFTs, gifts of stock, or gift in kind gifts.
Monthly *fees can be high de*pending on *your need and time f*rame.
Only provides support to children.
Donors can only raise up to $1 million. Limited amount of donor communication support.
Depending on your organization's budget, there might be cheaper options to raising your needed funds.
Does not provide access to social media.
Website is not easily navigable.
Provides limited services.
Only supports.

Giving Platforms Section 3 (C)

Provider name	Pros
Just Give	Helps individuals find charities to support. Supporters can write reviews on your organization.
missionfish.org	Exposure to eBay's global community. Sellers also have the option to send proceeds to their nonprofit of choice. Turn-key; good for purely volunteer-run organizations, like school or church committees.
modestneeds.com	Cheap platform option that allows you access to your donors' contact information.
Network for Good/ Donate Now	Donors have the option of covering the transaction fee. Volunteer network accessible to connect nonprofits to organizational efforts.
PayPal	Easy setup, accepts donations in 24 currencies, and has 24-hour support.
Razoo	Offers a mobile giving "widget" that allows donors to make gifts on the go.
SAGE	Sage allows supporters of organizations to share donation and event registration forms to anyone that would be interested in supporting their organization.
SeeYourImpact.org	Your donors get to see a picture and profile of the person or group they helped.
sixdegrees.org (see network for good)	You can give gift cards as gifts and individuals can then use the cards towards their charity of choice.
socialactions.com	Easy payment platform.
Uend.org	100% of your donation goes to your selected charitable organization. They cover the transaction fees.
universalgiving.org	No cost to set up services. Fees are only accessed by PayPal.
YourCause.com	Easy to use repository for nonprofit organizations and charitable efforts.

Cons
The minimum gift is $10.
Limited to raising money through eBay community. Would not replace more robust and customizable efforts.
Only provides support to low income individuals.
Does not accept FT/ACHs or Discover card.
Does not provided additional support services like donor communication, web analytics, etc.
Does not accept Discover cards or EFT/ ACHs.
There are few downsides to this provider. They offer an entire suite of essential and value added services at a affordable price for an established organization. This provider might not make sense though for a micro-fundraiser.
Does not offer support beyond acting as a giving platform.
Charity must be registered with Guidestar.
Lacks value added tools like donor communication support.
Only provides support to initatives focused on fighting poverty.
UniversalGiving.org supports a limited number of causes and organizations that are vetted throug their screen process.
Solely operates as a giving platform.

Appendix B

List of Charity
Evaluation Services

Charity Database Section 1 (A)

Provider	Sample Clients	Cost
BBB.org	Individuals and foundations who are seeking and reviewing nonprofits.	$0 for users/ $1,000–$15,000 sliding scale for nonprofits
bringlight.com	Individuals and foundations who are seeking and reviewing nonprofits.	$0
charitynavigator.org	Individuals and foundations who are seeking and reviewing nonprofits.	$0
charitywatch.org	Individuals and foundations who are seeking and reviewing nonprofits.	$40
donorschoose.org	Licensed teachers who are seeking additional funds for classroom projects.	$0
FoundationCenter.com	Individuals and foundations who are seeking and reviewing nonprofits.	$195- $1,295/ annual
givewell.net	Individuals and foundations who are seeking and reviewing nonprofits.	$0
Greatnonprofits.com	Donors and volunteers who are seeking to become more informed and nonprofits who wish to promote their efforts and impact.	$0
Guidestar.com	Crowdrise, Firstgiving, JustGive.org, Stratascope Inc.	$125 per report, $250 per month, $1,500 per year
independentcharities.org	McKinsey & Co., Macy's, 3M, AARP	$0
insidegood.com	Nonprofit leaders, volunteers, donors, job-seekers, and employees who wish to comment on their respective nonprofit organizations.	$0

Summary	Open Reviews	Form 990	Financial Statements	Tax-exempt Number	Giving Opportunities
Y	N	N	Y	N	N
Y	Y	N	N	N	Y
Y	Y	N	Y	N	Y
Y	N	N	Y	N	N
Y	Y	N	N	N	Y
Y	N	Y	Y	Y	N
Y	N	N	Y	N	N
Y	Y	N	N	N	N
Y	Y	Y	Y	Y	Y
Y	N	N	N	N	Y
N	Y	N	Y	N	N

Charity Database Section 1 (B)

Provider	Sample Clients	Cost
IntelligentPhilanthropy.com	Individuals, family offices and foundations who are seeking and reviewing nonprofits.	$59/$199/$1,995 dep. on # of users
MinistryWatch.com	Individuals and foundations who are seeking and reviewing nonprofits.	$0
Philanthropedia.com	Individuals and foundations who are seeking and reviewing nonprofits.	$0
samaritanguide.com	Individuals and foundations who are seeking and reviewing nonprofits.	$0
SmartGivers.org	Individuals and foundations who are seeking and reviewing nonprofits.	$0
wildlifedirect.org	Bloggers and individuals seeking opportunites to either support or fund raise for conservation projects.	$0

Summary	Open Reviews	Form 990	Financial Statements	Tax-exempt Number	Giving Opportunities
Y	N	N	Y	N	N
Y	N	N	Y	Y	Y
Y	N	N	Y	N	Y
Y	N	N	Y	N	N
Y	N	Y	Y	Y	N
N	Y	N	N	N	Y

Charity Database Section 2 (A)

Provider	Hosted Solutions	Web Services	Enterprise Data Integration	Matching & Verification
BBB.org	N	N	N	N
bringlight.com	N	N	N	N
charitynavigator.org	N	N	N	N
charitywatch.org	N	N	N	N
donorschoose.org	N	N	N	N
FoundationCenter.com	N	N	N	N
givewell.net	N	N	N	N

Pro's	Con's
BBB.org is a trusted third-party reveiwer for businesses and nonprofits. If an organization hosts the BBB logo on their website, you know they have been through a rigorious screening process. This website also provides a considerable amount of financial data to help assist individuals in their giving dicussions.	BBB does not provide any value added services such as direct giving opportunities, enterprise data integration, or web services.
Bringlight.com is free and offers a user-friendly wesite that tracks the giving to different projects.	This provider offers limited additional services.
Charity Navigator is an easy-to-use website with essential financial figures relating to overall revenue and expenses.	Charity Navigator does not provide additional analytical reporting or hosting services.
Offers third-party reviews and critiques of charitable and nonprofit organizations.	Charity Watch's website is not user-friendly and covers a limited number of organizations.
Provides teachers the opportunity to raise money for projects that fall outside of their budgets. The website is user-friendly and integrated with Facebook and Twitter to help increase chatter about your fundraising efforts.	The site only provides assistance to licensed teachers.
FoundationCenter provides an extensive database of over 100,000 grantmakers that includes their Form 990s.	The downside with FoundationCenter is that they only cover foundations and not traditional nonprofit organizations.
GiveWell.net provides users a considerable amount of detailed information regarding the activities and the financials of a nonprofit. The site also provides a range of cited sources to back their reviews.	GiveWell.net does not provide users the opportunity to give directly to the nonprofit that is being reviewed.

Charity Database Section 2 (B)

Provider	Hosted Solutions	Web Services	Enterprise Data Integration	Matching & Verification
Greatnonprofits.com	N	N	N	N
Guidestar.com	Y	Y	Y	Y
independentcharities.org	N	Y	N	N
insidegood.com	N	N	N	N
IntelligentPhilanthropy.com	N	Y	N	N
MinistryWatch.com	N	N	N	N
Philanthro-pedia.com	N	N	N	N

Pro's	Con's
GreatNonprofits.com provides a user-friendly platform for individuals to comment on their respective organizations that can then be posted on Facebook, Twitter, and LinkedIn.	The website does not provide supporting information like financials or Form 990s to help aid the individual in their decision-making process.
A premium provider who offers first-rate support services for donors, grantors, and nonprofits who are conducting research.	Guidestar does not provide giving opportunities on the website. The site and services only provide research.
IndependentCharities.com's main focus is to provide corporation employees free administrative, logistical, and fund distribution services to support employer giving programs.	IndependentCharities.com does not provide financial information on their member charities.
InsideGood.com's main focus is capturing supporters', employees', and volunteers' reviews of nonprofits. In doing so they provide an open dialogue for individuals to discuss the pros and cons of an organization.	To date only 209 nonprofits have been rated. The site also provides a limited amount of financial information.
Simple PDF produced from charity information and includes several years' worth of financials (to current available) summarized in table format; IP's assessment of the charity; and charity answers to "Expanded Drucker Questions." Strong international component; ability to search charity by "Nation served."	Newer service; therefore small database. Limited mainly to Christian nonprofits.
Includes recent financial summaries. Includes criticism of site itself. Promotes transparency. In-depth information at no cost.	Lacks 990s.
Philanthropedia.com offers user an extensive review of an organization's financials, operations, employee training, and collaboration with other organizations, as well as areas that need improvement.	The downside to Philanthropedia.com is that they only cover approximately 375 nonprofits so you might not be able to find information on the nonprofit you are researching.

Charity Database Section 2 (C)

Provider	Hosted Solutions	Web Services	Enterprise Data Integration	Matching & Verification
samaritanguide.com	N	N	N	N
SmartGivers.org	N	N	N	N
wildlifedirect.org	N	N	N	N

Pro's	Con's
SamaritanGuide.com provides a comprehensive review of an organization's mission, practices, and financials. They also offer charities the chance to win a $10,000 annual prize if the organization's work proves to be direct, personal, and accountable.	SamaritanGuide.com focuses mainly on private nonprofits who do not receive monies from government agencies. They also do not provide you the option to review or give directly to the nonprofit you are reviewing.
SmartGivers.org recognizes nonprofits who have demonstrated a commitment to accountability and openness by voluntarily participating in SmartGiver's screening process. In doing so this site is able to provide a considerable amount of supporting financial information for individual reviewers to consider.	SmartGivers.org does not provide additional value added reporting and hosting services.
For individuals interested in giving and connecting with conservation efforts across Africa, this is a great site.	Site only covers conservation efforts.

Index